LINCOLN CHRISTIAN COLLEGE

P9-CDH-278

ABSOLUTELY FREE!

A Biblical Reply
to Lordship Salvation

ABSOLUTELY FREE!

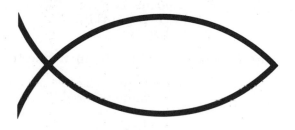

Zane C. Hodges

REDENCIÓN VIVA

Box 141167
Dallas, Texas 75214

Academie
Books Grand Rapids,
Michigan
Zondervan Publishing House

Absolutely Free!
Copyright © 1989 by Redención Viva

This title is copublished and codistributed by
Academie Books, an imprint of
Zondervan Publishing House
1415 Lake Drive, S.E.
Grand Rapids, Michigan 49506
in cooperation with and by permission of
Redención Viva
P. O. Box 141167
Dallas, TX 75214

Library of Congress Cataloging in Publication Data

Hodges, Zane Clark.
Absolutely Free!

Bibliography: p.
Includes indexes.
1. Salvation. 2. Faith. 3. Freedom (Theology).
4. Merit (Christianity). I. Title. II. Title:
Lordship salvation.
BT751.2.H56 1989   234   89-15181
ISBN 0-310-51960-8

All Scripture quotations are from the Holy Bible, New King
James Version. Copyright © 1979, 1980, 1982
by Thomas Nelson, Inc., Publishers.
Used by permission.

All rights reserved. No part of this publication may be
reproduced, stored in a retrieval system, or transmitted in any
form or by any means—electronic, mechanical, photocopy,
recording, or any other—except for brief quotations in printed
reviews, without the prior permission of the publisher.

Edited by Leonard G. Goss

Printed in the United States of America

89 90 91 92 93 94 / DH / 10 9 8 7 6 5 4 3 2 1

To my parents,

Z. C. and Virginia Hodges,

who understood before I did
that salvation is
absolutely free!

gratis

113971

Contents

Foreword

The church at Ephesus was in serious trouble when the apostle Paul called the elders together at Miletus and warned them:

> Therefore take heed to yourselves and to all the flock, over which the Holy Spirit has made you overseers, to shepherd the church of God which He purchased with His own blood. For I know this, that after my departure savage wolves will come in among you, not sparing the flock. Also from among yourselves men will rise up, speaking perverse things, to draw away disciples after themselves. Therefore watch, and remember that for three years I did not cease to warn everyone night and day with tears (Ac 20:28–31).

A problem that warranted warnings night and day with tears for three years was surely serious.

In much broader dimensions, however, the churches in America are in serious trouble, and the target of the attack is the very heart of our message, the nature of the gospel of redemption.

In the Ephesian situation, the attack was both from the outside—the savage wolf—and from the inside—men rising up speaking misleading things and drawing away disciples after themselves.

It is this latter problem that is ripping evangelicals apart today. Although there is general agreement on the problem—increasing profession of faith in Christ with decreasing demonstration of Christian moral and ethical values—there is broad disagreement about the solution. And in some cases the cures seem more dangerous than the disease.

One such suggested cure is popularly known as "lordship salvation," which in its earnest attempt to elevate the commitment level of God's people, seems to be undermining the very uniqueness of the gospel on which the church is built.

In defense of the purity of the gospel of grace, Zane Hodges has combined his years of careful biblical exposition with seasoned humility and simplicity to recapture a portrait of God's unconditional love. He does not engage in empty rhetoric nor biting polemic. There is no attack on individuals. Rather, he depends on the Spirit of God to use the repeated exposure of the words of God's revelation to bring understanding, edification, thanksgiving, and worship.

When you have finished *Absolutely Free!*, I trust that you will be able to join me in saying, "Thank you, Lord Jesus."

Earl D. Radmacher
President, Western Conservative Baptist Seminary
Portland, Oregon

Foreword

This book leads me to look back to the time when I came to trust the Lord Jesus Christ. It happened in an old building with a woodburning stove and handmade benches. But the true gospel was preached there every Sunday and every Friday night.

How easy it was for a boy of nine to understand the freeness of the gospel that was taught there. The gift of eternal life was received just by asking for it! But how soon we forget how we came to trust the Lord. We begin to put things into the gospel, things like "lordship," repentance, surrender, even baptism.

Absolutely Free! will challenge every Christian to look at what he or she is teaching today concerning the true gospel. In a time when all kinds of things are being taught, evangelical Christians must decide whether salvation is a free gift or not.

Zane Hodges has helped us in his other books. But this may be his best book yet. There are many important insights into how the truth of God works in us, both in salvation and in the Christian life. Some of these insights are found in the twelfth chapter on repentance.

Absolutely Free! is like a breath of fresh air. The truth it presents has always been here in the church, but just covered over. This book brushes away that cover and now we see God's truth once again.

Luis C. Rodriguez
Co-Pastor, Victor Street Bible Chapel
Dallas, Texas

Preface

Many years ago, as a teenage boy, I attended a series of evangelistic meetings in a small Baptist church in Hagerstown, Maryland. Although I was already saved, the meetings made a lasting impression on me as a young believer.

Not only was the offer of salvation presented at those meetings in beautiful simplicity, but the theme chorus fastened itself permanently on my heart. The words of the chorus were simple, but their truth was profound. The words were these:

> Absolutely free! Yes, it is
>   absolutely free!
> For God has given salvation,
>   absolutely free!
> Absolutely free! Yes, it is
>   absolutely free!
> For God has given His great salvation,
>   absolutely free!
>   —Author unknown

Four decades have passed since those meetings were held. But years of Bible study, in private as well as in a Christian college and in a theological seminary, have done nothing to diminish the loveliness of that chorus.

Nor have its resonances ceased to thrill me after years of preaching and teaching God's Word. Indeed, it has been my privilege to witness the power of this simple truth in the hearts and lives of many men and women, young and old.

Of course, the writer of the chorus knew whereof he spoke. His words are biblical to the core. In fact what he actually did was to capture in song the very essence of the Christian Gospel. He has set to music the most splendid invitation ever heard by man. And that invitation is nothing less than the offer proclaimed through John the apostle:

> Whoever desires, let him take the water of life freely (Rev 22:17).

This book is about that offer. It is first and foremost a tribute to the perfect freeness of God's saving grace. And it comes from the heart of a writer who can find no words adequate to describe so great a gift, but who worships his Savior for it.

In the following pages, whatever must be said to set this gospel in clear relief is said as plainly as possible. So marvelous a message should always be proclaimed without ambiguity and without compromise. It is worthy of nothing less than that.

But it is also worthy of much more. It is worthy of our lifelong devotion to the God who gave us His love so freely. And precisely because it is free, it powerfully motivates that very devotion.

I count it a privilege, therefore, to be numbered among those who believe that the moment of simple faith in Christ for eternal life is the very point at which God and human beings can meet. And in that moment of meeting, one's destiny is permanently settled and the miraculous life of eternity itself is created within. Out of a condition of spiritual death we pass into the sphere of spiritual life, with all the rich possibilities which that great transition brings with it.

Who can write worthily of such truth as this? Nevertheless, we will seek to do so to the extent that God is pleased to enable us. But there is one thing we do know: "The gift of God is eternal life in Christ Jesus our Lord" (Ro 6:23).

Or to put it another way: God's grace to sinful men and women is—both now and always—*absolutely free!*

1

INTRODUCTION: FATHER AND SON

1

Introduction:
Father and Son

In one of His most unforgettable parables, the Lord Jesus describes the spiritual awakening of the prodigal son in these words:

> And when he came to himself, he said, "How many of my father's hired servants have bread enough and to spare, and I perish with hunger! I will arise and go to my father, and will say to him, 'Father, I have sinned against heaven and before you, and I am no longer worthy to be called your son. Make me like one of your hired servants'" (Lk 15:17–19).

"This life is no good," the prodigal was saying to himself. "Even my father's paid servants are better off than I am! So why don't I go back, admit I was wrong and ask my dad to let me work for him?"

With His usual masterly skill, our Lord has aptly described thoughts that have often been found in the hearts of unsaved sinners. In particular, such thoughts may occur to people who have fallen into the depths of sin. Like the prodigal son himself, they decide that their present lifestyle is worthless.

They also realize that they need God. So they decide to turn back to him. But like the prodigal again, they often do not know on what terms they will be received.

They know, of course, that they have done wrong and grievously so. They are prepared to admit that to God. But they may also entertain the notion that they must work for Him in order to gain His acceptance.

On this point, the prodigal son was wrong. What he imagined was that he could strike a bargain with his father. If his dad would allow him to live at home, he would work for everything he got.

But that was not his father's idea at all! Instead, he was eagerly waiting for his son to come back to him. And he was fully prepared to receive him without any conditions at all.

Indeed, the father's loving acceptance would be granted absolutely free!

Thus the story continues: "And he arose and came to his father. But when he was still a great way off, his father saw him and had compassion, and ran and fell on his neck and kissed him" (Lk 15:20).

Not a word has yet escaped the lips of the boy! But already he has his father's total and unconditional acceptance.

It is only now that he speaks: "And the son said to him, 'Father, I have sinned against heaven and in your sight, and am no longer worthy to be called your son'" (15:21).

No doubt the prodigal is overwhelmed by so gracious a reception. Rightly, he feels utterly unworthy of such love. And so he now gives the first part of the little speech he had planned.

But he only gives *part* of that speech! The words, "Make me like one of your hired servants," are never spoken at all.

And no wonder! The son now realizes that the "bargain" he was planning to suggest is not relevant to an encounter like this. Obviously, he already has his dad's forgiveness and love. To speak such words now would be terribly crass and totally inappropriate.

The father's next words confirm this. The son had just expressed his unworthiness, and his dad responds to this by giving orders to his servants:

> Bring out the best robe and put it on him, and put a ring on his hand and sandals on his feet. And bring the fattened calf here and kill it, and let us eat and be merry; for this my son was dead and is alive again; he was lost and is found (15:22–24).

If by any chance the words, "Make me like one of your hired servants," still hovered on the boy's lips, he must now have quickly choked them back.

His father was not thinking about what his son could do for him. He was thinking instead of what he could now do for his son!

And it was as a son—not as a hired servant—that his father had received him. Nothing less than the best robe must be his along with the ring and the sandals. The party that followed did not celebrate the arrival of a new worker for the father's farm! The party celebrated the recovery of a lost son. It celebrated the coming to life of one who had formerly been dead.

And such indeed is the joy of heaven whenever a sinner, lost and dead in his sins, turns to God and is met by the unconditional love of a gracious heavenly Father.

But, tragically, the joy our Lord so richly described is slipping away from many in the evangelical church today. Instead of recognizing the freeness of God's saving love, many encumber it with conditions.

What is more, they even validate the prodigal son's original thoughts about making a bargain with his dad.[1] According to them, the father would not have received his son if his son had not been willing to serve! The tragic wrongness of this view cannot be stressed too much.

Lordship Salvation

It would be difficult to imagine a conversation like this between a father and his son:

Son: "Dad, am I *really* your son, or am I only adopted?"

Father: "Well, young man, it depends on how you behave. If you really are my son, you will show this by doing the things I tell you to do. If you have my nature inside of you, you can't help but be obedient."

Son: "But what if I disobey you a lot, Dad?"

Father: "Then you have every reason to doubt that you are truly my son!"

What sort of a father would talk to his son like that? Would he not rightly be accused of cruelty for dealing in this fashion with the anxieties of his child? At a moment like this, is not his child's most urgent need a sense of acceptance and parental love?

But to withhold this acceptance, in order to secure his boy's obedience, is to traffic in rejection and fear.

Yet, strangely enough, this is the kind of dialogue some Christian teachers apparently feel would be appropriate between God and man. According to them, if a person wonders whether he is a Christian or not, he ought to be told to look for evidence of this in his behavior.[2]

It is dangerous, these teachers assert, to offer someone the assurance that they are accepted with God apart from the issue of obedience. For them, there is no such thing as an unconditional love of God that is not, in some way, performance-related.

This is the tragedy of the evangelical church today. To an alarming degree it has lost touch with the unconditional love of God. To an amazing extent, it has become blind to the heart of a loving Father who is waiting, like the father of the prodigal son, to embrace sinners with His total acceptance and with His lavish forgiveness.

And even if the repenting sinner thinks he should pledge lifelong service to the God whom he has offended, the Father will not allow such a pledge to be a part of His gracious acceptance of the offender!

But many evangelicals today have forgotten this truth. Indeed, they even deny it. The most obvious result has been the spread of what is frequently called "lordship salvation." This is the view that *a commitment to obedience must be a part of true spiritual conversion.*[3] But beneath the surface lie all the hideous fruits of this disastrous way of thinking.

Eternity alone will reveal how many thousands of people have been deprived of their assurance by this teaching and have been brought into the bondage of fear in their relationship to God.

Instead of promoting holiness, the doctrine of lordship salvation destroys the very foundation on which true holiness must be built. By returning to the principles of the law, it has forfeited the spiritual power of grace.

A *Judgmental Spirit*

As if the results already mentioned were not enough, lordship salvation also promotes a judgmental and pharisaical spirit within the church. How tempting it is to our sinful flesh to believe that we have a right to say to a failing professing believer, "You really are not good enough to be on your way to heaven"!

Of course, this point is rarely put in so stark a form. But no matter how carefully the matter is disguised in religious jargon, or obscured by sophisticated theology, the sad fact remains the same. Lordship teaching reserves to itself the right to strip professing Christians of their claims to faith and to consign such people to the ranks of the lost.

To be sure, there is much reason to think that there are multitudes of people in churches today who have never really been saved. But this is due to their failure to understand the gospel offer, or to accept it.[4] The fact that a person falls below the moral standards laid down in God's Word is always tragic and deplorable. But it is not necessarily a proof that one is also unsaved. Is there any Christian who does not have areas of failure which he or she must seek God's grace to overcome?

But lordship thought is not satisfied simply to insist that some conversion experiences are not valid. Nearly everyone would agree to that. Instead, lordship doctrine even goes so far as to disallow an individual's claim to personal trust in Christ on the grounds that their life is so unworthy that the claim could not be true.

But the price paid for the privilege of making this kind of judgment is enormously high. The cost is nothing less than a radical rewriting of the gospel proclaimed by our Lord and by His apostles. And this leads to a complete reshaping of the concept of "saving faith." The result is that what passes for faith in lordship thought is no longer recognizable as the biblical quality that goes by the same name.

It may even be said that lordship salvation throws a veil of obscurity over the entire New Testament revelation. In the process, the marvelous truth of justification by faith, apart from works, recedes into shadows not unlike those which darkened the days before the Reformation. What replaces this doctrine is a kind of faith/works synthesis which differs only insignificantly from official Roman Catholic dogma.[5]

Conclusion

It goes without saying that an error of this magnitude cannot be dismissed as irrelevant to the life of the church.

Neither can it be ignored in the vain hope that it will go away of its own accord. Instead, it must be faced and responded to by all who hold dear the gospel of God's saving grace. To do less would be to fail the Lord, and to fail His people, and, indeed, to fail the world for which He died.

For if the church itself cannot decide on the nature of the message it is called to proclaim, how can lost men and women be brought into living touch with the redeeming love of God? And "if the trumpet makes an uncertain sound, who will prepare himself for battle?" (1Co 14:8).

It is true, of course, that there is something distasteful about religious controversy. This author does not like it at all. Nevertheless, it must be kept in mind that several New Testament books apparently grew out of some kind of doctrinal difficulty or confusion.

Paul's white-hot letter to the Galatians most readily comes to mind. But one might also think of Colossians, 2 Thessalonians, 1 Timothy, 2 Peter, 1 and 2 John, and Jude. Were it not for the difficulties that produced them, we would not have these valuable epistles at all.

So God knows how to use controversy to advance His own interests and to highlight His own truth.

The same God who commanded light to shine on the first day of Creation proceeded next to divide that light from the darkness around it. Finally, He gave them both their proper names, for "God called the light Day, and the darkness He called Night" (Ge 1:3–5).

And God has always done this with the light of His truth. First He reveals it—He commands it to shine. But He also divides this light from the encroaching darkness all around it, calling each by its true name. And in the religious realm, He calls their names truth and error!

This, then, is the up-side of religious controversy. It is a tool in the hands of the living God to set His truth more sharply in focus. Undesirable though it is, in itself, controversy serves to make God's truth more clearly distinct from the error that would distort and hide it.

It is to be hoped that, by the grace of God, the debate over lordship salvation will accomplish these very objectives in our own day and time. And should that happen, God's people would have reason to be grateful indeed.

After all, what could be more profitable to the church than to be impressed all over again with the grand simplicity of God's saving grace? And what could be better for the world to which we are called to proclaim this grace?

For if *we've* got it straight, we can then *tell* it straight!

2

FAITH MEANS JUST THAT—FAITH!

2

Faith Means Just
That—Faith!

It would be hard to find a statement in the Bible more superbly simple than the words of the Lord Jesus Christ when he said:

Most assuredly, I say to you, he who believes in Me has everlasting life (Jn 6:47).

So simple, in fact, is this announcement, that even relatively young children are able to understand it. Certainly the average person on the street can understand it. Its directness and clarity are sublime.

In fact, it is statements like this one that show how anxious God is to make His offer of salvation plain. Although there are subjects in the Bible that are hard to understand—Peter himself said so (2Pe 3:16)—the way of salvation is not one of them.

Indeed, multitudes of men and women, young and old, from every walk of life, have found Christ through verses just as simple as this one.

Yet though the average person, and even a child, can grasp John 6:47, some Christian teachers and theologians do not!

In what must certainly be one of the worst distortions of the Bible in our day, the meaning of our Lord's words are radically transformed by those who hold to lordship salvation. From being a model of simplicity, the Savior's statement is reduced to incomprehensible obscurity.

What He *really* meant by these words—so we are told—is something like this:

> Most assuredly, I say to you, he who *repents, believes, and submits totally to my will*, has everlasting life.

In support of this obvious revision of the text, we are assured that all the additional ideas are contained implicitly within the word "believe." If only we understood the biblical concept of "saving faith," it is claimed, then we would see the validity of this way of understanding Jesus' words.[1]

What a surprise! Who would ever have guessed it? Were it not for the doctrine of saving faith which is promoted by lordship theology, what reader would ever have understood our Lord in this way? Indeed, he or she could have searched the entirety of John's gospel repeatedly and never found even one reference to repentance, much less a reference to surrender or submission as a condition for eternal life. But, of course, they would find the word "believe" many, many times!

These observations already carry on their face a refutation of lordship thought. The fact is that John's gospel is *the only book in the New Testament* which plainly declares that it was written with an evangelistic purpose in view. Thus, in John 20:30–31, the inspired Evangelist says:

> And truly Jesus did many other signs in the presence of His disciples, which are not written in this book; but these are written that you may believe that Jesus is the Christ, the Son of God, and that believing you may have life in His name.

Yet, despite this clearly stated aim to bring men to saving faith, John's gospel is as far from articulating lordship salvation as day is far from night!

Something has gone wrong in the evangelical world when a doctrine can be tolerated that so plainly clashes with the repeated statements of the fourth evangelist. What is the problem here? Where are the roots of this confusion?

What Is Saving Faith?

Perhaps the most fundamental answer to such questions is to say that large sections of the Christian church have quietly yielded to a process that has turned the meaning of faith upside down.

Over a period of many years the idea has gained ground that true saving faith is somehow distinguishable from false kinds of faith, primarily by means of its results or "fruits."[2]

Thus two men might believe exactly the same things in terms of content, yet if one of them exhibited what seemed to be a "fruitless" Christian experience, his faith would be condemned as "intellectual assent," or "head belief" over against "heart belief." In a word, his faith was false faith—it was faith that did not, and could not, save.

With such ideas as these, the ground was prepared for full-fledged lordship theology. It remained for lordship thinkers to take the matter one step further.

What was really missing in false faith, so they affirmed, were the elements of true repentance and submission to God. Thus, saving faith ought not to be defined in terms of trust alone, but also in terms of commitment to the will of God. In the absence of this kind of submission, they insisted, one could not describe his faith as biblical saving faith.

If ever there existed a theological Trojan horse, this point of view is it!

Under cover of a completely insupportable definition of saving faith, lordship teaching introduces into the Christian church a doctrine of salvation which was unknown to the New Testament authors. It transforms the offer of a free gift of eternal life into a "contract" between the sinner and God, and it turns the joy of Christian living into a grueling effort to verify our faith and our acceptance before God. As theology, it is a complete disaster.

But it is also nonsense. A little reflection will show this.

In every other sphere of life, except religion, we do not puzzle ourselves with introspective questions about the "nature" of our faith. For example, if I say to someone, "Do you believe that the President will do what he has promised?" I could expect any one of three possible answers. One answer might be, "Yes, I do." Another might be, "No, I don't." But my respondent might also reply, "I'm not sure," or, "I don't know."

There is nothing complicated about this exchange. Two of the three answers reveal a lack of trust in the President. The answer, "No, I don't," indicates positive disbelief of the President's reliability. The reply, "I'm not sure," indicates uncertainty about the integrity of the President. Only the response, "Yes, I do," indicates faith or trust.

Of course, my respondent could be lying to me when he says, "Yes, I do." I might even know him well enough to say, "You're putting me on, aren't you? You don't really trust the President at all, do you?"

But it is certainly not likely that I would say, "What is the nature of this faith you have in the President? Would you now go out and break a law? And if you did, would that not raise a question about whether you really trust him?"

Such a question would be absurd. My respondent would have every reason to think I was joking. And if he took me seriously, he would have a perfect right to reply, "What has my breaking a law got to do with my firm conviction that I can trust the President in anything he says?"

Clearly, we all operate at the level of common sense when we talk about faith as it relates to everyday life. It is only when we discuss this subject in religion that we tend to check our common sense at the door.[3]

Indeed, in ordinary human life, the concept of "false faith" would arise only rarely. What would such an expression mean in normal conversation? Would it not have to mean something like "misplaced faith" or "pretended faith"? A person who had such a faith might be mistaken in believing what they do. His or her actual convictions might be false. Or they might only be pretending to a conviction, or confidence, that they did not in reality possess.

But "false faith" would never refer to a real conviction or trust which somehow fell below some imaginary standard which measured its results!

Let it be clearly stated here that English words like to "believe," or "faith" function as fully adequate equivalents to their Greek counterparts. There is not some hidden residue of meaning in the Greek words that is not conveyed by their normal English renderings. Although some have affirmed that there is, this claim betrays an inadequate or misguided view of biblical linguistics.[4]

It follows that a Greek reader who met the words "he who believes in Me has everlasting life," would understand the word "believe" exactly as we do. The reader *most certainly* would not understand this word to imply submission, surrender, repentance, or anything else of this sort. For those readers, as for us, "to believe" meant "to believe."

Surely it is one of the conceits of modern theology to suppose that we can define away simple terms like "belief" and "unbelief" and replace their obvious meanings with complicated elaborations. The confusion produced by this sort of process has a pervasive influence in the church today.

The solution, however, is to return to the plain meaning of the biblical text.

Intellectual Assent

Among the most frequent code words encountered in lordship teaching are those found in expressions like "cheap grace," "easy believism," and "intellectual assent." All three of these phrases are usually used to disparage the idea that eternal life can be obtained by a simple act of trust in Christ. All three represent a seriously distorted assessment of the issues involved.

Naturally the saving grace of God could never be described as "cheap" in the negative sense this word often has. The fact is that God paid an enormous price—the death of His Son—to make His grace available to us. Simply because the offer of grace is made free of charge to *us* does not transform that grace into something "cheap" or valueless.

After all, when the Bible can say, "And whoever desires, let him take the water of life freely" (Rev 22:17), we obviously are not talking about something "cheap"—even in the positive sense of that word. We are talking, rather, about something which is absolutely free!

Equally objectionable is the phrase "easy believism." Presumably the opposite would be "hard believism." And if

any system of thought teaches "hard believism," lordship
salvation certainly does.

As we have just noted, lordship thought abandons the
straightforward meaning of the word "believe" and fills the
concept of saving faith with illegitimate complications. The
result is that the saving transaction is made much more
complex than it actually is. But salvation really *is* simple and,
in that sense, it is easy! After all, what could be simpler than
to "take the water of life freely."

But the most misleading of all the lordship code-word
expressions is the phrase "intellectual (or, mental) assent."

Usually what is implied by this phrase is a type of belief
that is emotionally and volitionally remote and disinterested.
Words like "intellectual" or "mental" are primarily to blame
for this.

If I say, "That man has only an intellectual interest in
politics," I have implied that his interest is too detached and
academic. The same effect is produced in English when I
say, "He has only given the proposition his mental assent."
Again, I am suggesting detachment and personal disinterest.

But suppose I say, "I made an important point, and he
assented." Then the effect is different. I imply by these
words a meaningful agreement with what I have said. And
there is no negative undertone of any kind.

Clearly, the terms "intellectual" and "mental" cause the
trouble.

Of course, "intellectual" can mean nothing more than "of
or pertaining to the intellect," and need not carry any
negative overtones at all. But the fact remains that in many of
its everyday uses it does carry these overtones. Thus the
expression "intellectual assent" already has a prejudicial
connotation for most English speakers. The phrase immediately sounds as if it is in some way undesirable.

In this context, we should discard words like mental or
intellectual altogether. The Bible knows nothing about an
intellectual faith as over against some other kind of faith (like
emotional or volitional).[5] What the Bible does recognize is
the obvious distinction between faith and unbelief!

No one needs to be a psychologist to understand what faith
is. Still less do we need to resort to "pop psychology" to

explain it. It is an unproductive waste of time to employ the popular categories—intellect, emotion, or will—as a way of analyzing the mechanics of faith.[6] Such discussions lie far outside the boundaries of biblical thought. People know whether they believe something or not, and that is the real issue where God is concerned.

But lordship salvation drives its adherents into a psychological shadowland. We are told that true faith has volitional and emotional elements. But we might ask: In what sense?

Have we not all at some time been compelled by facts to believe something we did not wish to believe? Did we not, in a sense, believe against our will? Was that not even the case with Saul of Tarsus on the road to Damascus? And is it not equally true that we often believe things without any discernible emotional response to them, while at other times we are overwhelmed with emotion?

Such questions show how precarious and contradictory are the notions about faith which arise out of popular psychology.

The one thing we cannot do, however, is to believe something we don't know about. That is why the apostle Paul declared quite plainly, "And how shall they believe in Him of whom they have not heard?" (Ro 10:14). And he added appropriately, "So then faith comes by hearing, and hearing by the word of God" (10:17).

Does that involve the intellect? Of course! But is it *mere* intellectual assent? Of course *not*! To describe faith that way is to demean it as a trivial, academic exercise, when in fact it is no such thing.

What faith really is, in biblical language, is receiving the testimony of God. It is the *inward conviction* that what God says to us in the gospel is true. That—and that alone—is saving faith.[7]

It was precisely this concept of saving faith which so clearly shaped the words of the apostle John when he wrote:

If we receive the witness of men, the witness of God is greater; for this is the witness of God which He has testified of His Son. He who believes in the Son of God has the witness in himself; he who does not believe God has made Him a liar, because he has not believed the testimony that God has given of His Son. And this is the testimony: that God has given us eternal life, and this life is in His Son. He who has the Son has life; he who does not have the Son of God does not have life. These things I have written to you who believe in the name of the Son of God, that you may know that you have eternal life . . . (1Jn 5:9–13a).

How delightfully free this is of needless complications. Since we often accept human testimony, how much more ought we to accept divine testimony? To do this is to possess that testimony inwardly—within ourselves. The opposite of this—unbelief—is to make God out to be a liar.

Moreover, the divine testimony announces the gift of life that God gives in His Son, so that this life and the Son Himself are possessed together. Consequently, the original readers who have believed have God's word for it that eternal life is theirs. His own infinitely credible testimony is the grounds for their personal assurance!

And when a person has God's word for it, they have no need to seek assurance elsewhere.

Conclusion

In a justly famous passage about Abraham, the great biblical model of saving faith, Paul writes these words: "For what does the Scripture say? 'Abraham believed God, and it was counted to him for righteousness'" (Ro 4:3).

The utter simplicity of this should be apparent to all. Abraham trusted God's Word to him—he believed what God said—and this act of trust was put down to his account as righteousness. In other words, he was justified by faith.

Faith, then, is taking God at His Word. Saving faith is taking God at His Word in the gospel. It is nothing less than this. But it is also nothing more.

The effort to make it more is a tragic blemish on the history of the Christian church. The roots of this effort run deep into certain types of post-Reformation thought.[8] And in the English-speaking world, this radically altered concept of saving faith can with considerable fairness be described as Puritan theology. Lordship salvation, in its best known contemporary form, simply popularizes the Puritanism to which it is heir.[9]

But today, as always, when the Scriptures are permitted to speak for themselves—and when the church has ears prepared to hear them—the simplicity and freeness of salvation can reemerge as a vital force in the consciousness of God's people.

Nothing is more desirable than this result. But for such an aim to be realized, there is one thing we must be most careful to do. We must not fail at this crucial point. Simply stated, we must allow faith to be just that—faith.

3

DO YOU BELIEVE THIS?

3

Do You Believe This?

At a tragic moment in the life of Martha of Bethany, who had lost her brother Lazarus in death, the Lord Jesus Christ confronts her with a majestic claim. He says to her:

I am the resurrection and the life. He who believes in Me, though he may die, he shall live. And whoever lives and believes in Me shall never die (Jn 11:25–26).

He then adds a decisive question: "Do you believe this?" (11:26).

It is often claimed by those who teach lordship salvation that saving faith cannot be merely "believing facts." But this assertion is both misconceived and clearly wrong. It simply cannot stand up under biblical examination.

In His exchange with Martha, the Lord Jesus announced some staggering *facts*. He declares that He is both the Resurrection and the Life. Moreover, He proclaims to her His ability to guarantee the eternal destiny of anyone who believes in Him. If they die, He will raise them up. If they are alive, since He gives eternal life, there is a sense in which they do not die at all.

Nothing is trivial about any of these facts. Indeed, they are challenging beyond description.

Jesus stands before Martha in a fully human body. Yet He asks her whether she accepts realities about Himself that were completely invisible to her eyes, and which no other individual could have claimed without being guilty of

37

blasphemy. For Martha to believe facts like these would indeed be an impressive exercise of faith!

Faith and Facts

It is one of the tragic aspects of evangelical thought today that we have lost much of our appreciation for the majesty of simple faith in Christ. Although we live in an increasingly pagan world, where even belief in the existence of God is in decline, our esteem for the wonder of childlike trust in God is steadily eroding.

The New Testament does not share our modern point of view. The writers of Scripture knew perfectly well how hostile their environment was to the acceptance of Christian truth. They were in no way inclined to depreciate the worth of "believing the facts" about the Son of God. They recognized clearly how difficult that was for both Jew and Gentile alike.

It goes without saying, then, that the reply of Martha to our Lord deserves the very highest praise. For in response to the Savior's question, "Do you believe this?" she gives this answer: "Yes, Lord, I believe that You are the Christ, the Son of God, who is to come into the world" (Jn 11:27).

We need not ask why the apostle John has included this reply in his book. The reason is obvious! Martha is stating her belief in the very facts which John wishes all his readers to believe as well. For in the announcement of his purpose for writing, John clearly states:

> And truly Jesus did many other signs in the presence of His disciples, which are not written in this book; but these are written that you may believe *that Jesus is the Christ, the Son of God*, and that believing you may have life in His name (Jn 20:30–31; italics added).

Let there be no mistaking that indeed we are talking about "believing facts." Jesus said, "Do you believe *this*?" and Martha replies, "I believe *that You are* . . . ." And John wants his readers to "believe *that Jesus is* . . . ." The content of the faith under discussion is unmistakably factual.

But there is more to the exchange between Jesus and

Martha than this. The facts presented to her by the Lord are more than great facts. They are *saving* facts. That is, they are *divinely revealed facts which are to be believed for salvation.* Thus, Jesus' words to Martha are John's way of telling us what it means to believe that Jesus is the Christ, the Son of God.

Naturally, there are many people in the modern world who would claim to believe that Jesus is God's Son. For such people it goes almost without saying that He is also "the Christ." "After all," they might say, "isn't that His name?"

But if they were asked whether Jesus guarantees resurrection and eternal life to people on the simple basis of faith, their reply might very well be negative. "Of course not," they might say, "you also have to live right to get eternal life!" And in so saying, they would plainly disclose that they *did not believe* what the Savior asked Martha to believe.

Not all facts about God are saving facts. To believe, for example, in the unity of God (that God is One) saves no one. Every orthodox Jew in the Roman world believed *that*. So in fact, claims an opponent of James, do the demons (Jas 2:19). To be sure, the unity of God is glorious Christian truth. But it does not contain within itself the truth of the gospel.

But to believe that Jesus is the Christ—*in John's sense of that term*—is to believe saving truth. It is, in fact, to believe the very truth that Martha of Bethany believed. To put it as simply as possible, Jesus was asking Martha whether she *believed* that He fully guaranteed the eternal destiny of every *believer*. That was the same as asking if this great truth applied to *her* as well! And Martha affirmed that it did by affirming her conviction about who He was.

Thus, by believing the amazing facts about the person of Christ, Martha was *trusting* Him. She was placing her eternal destiny in His hands. If she was wrong about who He was, then her faith was sadly misplaced. But if she was right about this—and she was—then resurrection and eternal life were a certainty for her. She had Jesus' own word for it.

Everything depended on the *truth* of what she believed. It was not at all a question of what *kind* of faith she had. She either believed this or she didn't. It was as simple as that.

Faith as Appropriation

From all that has been said it should be clear that there is nothing wrong with "believing facts"—if those facts are true. And equally there is nothing wrong with "believing facts" in order to be saved—if those facts are indeed *saving truth*. But this leads quite naturally to a further observation.

Martha believed the facts about Jesus which it was necessary for her to believe in order to be saved. But in so doing she had actually *appropriated* the gift of eternal life.

To be sure, this occasion is not the point at which Martha originally believed. It was not the point at which she received eternal life. Instead, her Lord is asking her to articulate a faith which she already possessed.

That would be good for her. The death of her beloved brother had cast its dark shadow over her life. She needed to be reminded—she needed to express—her confidence in the One who vanquishes death for every person who believes in Him.

But clearly, that confidence of hers had been nothing less than a personal appropriation of saving truth. She had received the testimony of God about His Son (1Jn 5:9–13). And in so doing, she had appropriated eternal life itself.

No wonder, then, that in one of the most fundamental passages in his entire gospel, John presents saving faith as an act of appropriation. The passage in question, of course, is the unforgettable interview between Jesus and the Samaritan woman. It was Jesus who set the direction for their conversation with these words: "If you knew the gift of God, and who it is who says to you, 'Give Me a drink,' you would have asked Him, and He would have given you living water" (Jn 4:10).

"What you need to do," our Lord is saying, "is to *appropriate* something which I want to give you. But to do that, you need to know certain facts. You need to know what God's *gift* is, and you need to know who *I* am."

Could anything be clearer or more simple? This sin-burdened woman could not obtain eternal life unless she obtained crucial information. She needed to know something about this offer, and she needed to know something about the Person who was placing the offer before her.

The whole conversation that follows is designed to provide her with the needed information. God's gift was the water of life (4:13–14). It was not, as she supposed at first, the kind of water that would satisfy her *physical* thirst (4:15). Rather, it was water designed to meet her *spiritual* thirst, for the woman was a guilty sinner (4:16–18).

But that was only half of the truth she needed to know. She also needed to identify the Person who was speaking to her. Jesus deftly directs her toward that goal as well.

The woman is stung by the Lord's unexpected exposure of her barren life. Swiftly she changes the subject to religion in general. But she has to admit that the Person before her must surely be a prophet (4:19–20).

Yet He was much more than that! And in the impressive words that Jesus speaks to her in response (4:21–24), she catches a glimpse of something even greater than prophecy. So she says: "I know that Messiah is coming (who is called Christ). When He comes, He will tell us all things" (Jn 4:25).

The Savior's reply is brief and definitive: "I who speak to you am He" (4:26). And with this astounding claim the interview concludes.

Did the woman believe this claim? Of course she did. Naturally, in a village where her reputation stood so low, she must speak cautiously ("Could this be the Christ?"—4:29).[1] But the men to whom she bore witness knew she believed it (4:42). And though they disliked giving her any credit, they believed it too.

In fact, their statement of faith expresses exactly the conviction we have also seen Martha express. They say: "Now we believe, not because of what you said, for we have heard for ourselves and know that this is indeed *the Christ, the Savior of the world*" (Jn 4:42; italics added).

They believed a fact, but what a magnificent fact it was! This humble Jewish traveler was God's Christ! He was therefore also the Savior of the world—and that included Samaritans! In short, He was the Giver of eternal life to sinful people.

It has often been noticed that our Lord speaks the final

words in the conversation with the woman from Sychar. The words "I . . . am He" are not followed by a request from her for the true living water. Indeed she says nothing at all to *Him* . What she now has to say is for the men of her village.

But the transaction of which Jesus spoke to her has occurred nevertheless. John 4:10 had come to pass.

The woman had said: "I know that Messiah is coming . . . When He comes, He will tell us all things" (4:25). But these words are in reality a request. They mean something like this: "Please tell me! Are you the coming Messiah? Are you, in fact, the Savior of the world?"

So she had asked, as Jesus said she would. Therefore He gave, as He said *He* would. And His response—His gift—is the saving truth of the entire gospel of John: "I who speak to you am He" (4:26). Or, to rephrase it, Jesus replied: "I am the Christ, the Savior of the world!"

Thus, when the woman received this saving truth in faith, she received nothing less than the gift of God. God's testimony about His Son—His *living Word*—was now within her. Her faith was her act of appropriation. By it she had come into possession of the supernatural water of everlasting life.

Conclusion

In the closing chapter of his first epistle, the apostle John wrote as follows: "Whoever believes that Jesus is the Christ is born of God" (1Jn 5:1). This is as plain as it possibly could be. It is also completely harmonious with what we have just seen in John's gospel.[2]

The truth that Jesus is the Christ—the truth that He is the Giver of eternal life to every believer—is saving truth. Belief in this truth produces immediate—and permanent—new birth.

It follows, therefore, that there is no such thing as believing the saving message without possessing eternal life at the same time. "Everyone"—not just some or many—but "Everyone who believes that Jesus is the Christ is born of God." *There are no exceptions at all.*

So states the apostle.

But the superb simplicity of all this is lost on many modern evangelicals. Indeed, they are frightened by it, and they are tempted to evade it by invoking some special definition of saving faith. In the process, they cloud beyond hope the biblical doctrine of faith and distort in a tragic way the biblical message of grace.

In fact, in a real sense, they are trying to do God's work for Him. But when we do that, it is always a serious mistake and most often it is also disastrous. In this case, it certainly is disastrous.

Why this is so is the subject of the next chapter.

4

WHAT REALLY HAPPENED?

4

What Really Happened?

James, the half brother of our Lord, has written a classic and beautiful passage on the subject of new birth. He begins by speaking eloquently of God's wonderful capacity to give. He says: "Every good gift and every perfect gift is from above, and comes down from the Father of lights, with whom there is no variation or shadow of turning" (Jas 1:17).

Then, as a magnificent example of God's gift-giving ability, he adds: "Of His own will He brought us forth by the word of truth, that we might be a kind of firstfruits of His creatures" (Jas 1:18).

The words of James generously repay our closest attention. He is speaking here about the very gift which Jesus offered to the Samaritan woman. And, like our Lord, James is talking about a miracle wrought by God's truth: "He brought us forth by the word of truth."

In the contemporary church, however, confidence in the miraculous power of God's truth has sharply decreased. Lordship salvation teachers express alarm when the gospel is presented to men as a gift that is absolutely free. Instead of bowing before the immense generosity of God, they slander this offer as an expression of "cheap grace" or "easy believism."

No doubt many of them are sincerely concerned about what they perceive to be the low moral state of the professing church. But the cure which they propose is far worse than the disease they believe they have diagnosed.

Let it be said clearly that the addition of stringent conditions to the terms of salvation is no solution at all. Indeed, it is utterly counterproductive. What it will do, in fact, is to bring into the church multitudes of people who are strangers to the grace of God. For those already in the church, it will cloud the message of salvation and destroy their grounds of assurance.

In the wake of such an impact as this will come discouragement, defeat, and despair. These results are already being felt today in congregations where lordship salvation is preached.

When all is said and done, therefore, there is simply no substitute for the real miracle of new birth.

It Takes a Miracle

With memorable words a songwriter has written,

> It took a miracle to put the stars in place,
> It took a miracle to hang the world in space;
> But when He saved my soul,
> Cleansed and made me whole,
> It took a miracle of love and grace!
> —John W. Peterson
> *It Took A Miracle*

These words are true because they are also biblical.

We have already seen that the apostle John affirmed that receiving the testimony of God about His Son was having the testimony within ourselves (1Jn 5:9–10). With this we might well compare the declaration of the apostle Peter that we are "born again, not of corruptible seed but incorruptible, through the word of God which lives and abides forever" (1Pe 1:23). Shortly thereafter Peter adds, "And this is the word which by the gospel was preached to you" (1:25).

It is the consistent testimony of the New Testament Scriptures that God's Word in the gospel is what produces the miracle of regeneration. It—and it alone—is the powerful, life-giving seed which takes root in the human heart when that Word is received there in faith.

That is why it is really nonsense to deny that true faith can be directed toward "facts." For if the "facts" in question constitute God's saving message to men and women, then those facts are God's truth. Those facts are embodied and expressed in God's Word. And where God's Word is, there also is God's power.

But there is no power in man's word. And that is precisely what lordship salvation really is. Like strict religionists since the dawn of time, lordship thinkers feel that one must somehow "measure up" if he expects to attain eternal well-being. It is foreign to them that God's love can embrace sinful people unconditionally, with no binding requirements attached at all.

But the unconditionality of God's grace is what distinguishes God's saving Word so sharply from the word of man. How plainly this comes through in a text that we already have referred to several times: "And the Spirit and the bride say, 'Come!' And let him who hears say, 'Come!' And let him who thirsts come. And whoever desires, let him take the water of life freely" (Rev 22:17).

What an unmistakable message is conveyed in these words. If anyone is simply thirsty, he can take this water. But wait! Perhaps even *that* is too strong. So the Spirit adds, "whoever desires"—whoever wants to!—let him take this water without obligation. Let him take it freely.

And what happens to those who appropriate that water? What happens to those who believe this invitation?

A *miracle* happens to them. They are born again. New life is imparted to them. And in the possession of that life, they possess also God's Son (1Jn 5:12). Indeed, *He is that life* (1Jn 5:20c), and thus He Himself lives within them (Col 1:27).

How was this miracle accomplished in them? By the Word of God that lives and abides forever. Or, as James would say, "Of His own will He brought us forth by the word of truth."

It Brings Assurance

Yet another lovely song has left its words indelibly impressed on the soul of the church:

Blessed assurance, Jesus is mine!
Oh, what a foretaste of glory divine!
Heir of salvation, purchase of God,
Born of His Spirit, washed in His blood.
          —Fanny J. Crosby and Mrs. J.F. Knapp
          Blessed Assurance

The women who gave us this hymn obviously had grasped the very core of the biblical gospel. Their words and music are an undying tribute to the essence of the message of grace. Simply put, that message brings with it the assurance of salvation.

But how, indeed, is this assurance conveyed? The answer by now should be obvious. The same miracle-working Word which regenerates also imparts assurance to the heart that believes. Indeed, the two things are both simultaneous and inseparable.

Or to put it another way, when a person believes, that person has assurance of life eternal. How could it be otherwise? Think, for example, of the words of Jesus:

Most assuredly, I say to you, he who hears My word and believes in Him who sent Me has everlasting life, and shall not come into judgment, but has passed from death into life (Jn 5:24).

This is extremely clear. The believer, says our Lord, has eternal life. Moreover, he will not come into judgment. In fact, he has already passed out of death into life. And to believe His Word is to believe these things too!

Thus it is utterly impossible for us to give credence to the gospel message without knowing that we are saved. For that message carries its own guarantee along with it. Therefore, to doubt the guarantee of eternal life is to doubt the message itself.

In short, if I do not believe that I am saved, I do not believe the offer that God has made to me.[1]

That brings us back to Martha. When Martha declared that she believed Jesus to be "the Christ, the Son of God" (Jn 11:27), she was responding to the words, "Do you believe this?"

But behind the word "this" lay an important claim that

Jesus had made. In fact, in two ways He told her that He guaranteed the eternal destiny of every believer. First, He said: "He who believes in me, though he may die, he shall live" (Jn 11:25).

And, second, He said, "And whoever lives and believes in Me shall never die" (Jn 11:26).

Both of these great declarations are included in the word "this" when Jesus says, "Do you believe *this*?" It follows that if Martha believed "this," she believed "this" about herself too.

Indeed, to deny "this" for herself would have been to deny that "*whoever* lives and believes in Me shall never die." But Martha believed and, in so doing, she knew that she, too, would never die. In a word, like all believers, at the moment of saving faith Martha *knew* that she had eternal life.

This is not to say, however, that later on Martha could not have doubted this truth. Even John the Baptist doubted (Lk 7:18–20). But it is to say this: a person who has *never been sure* of eternal life has *never believed* the saving message of God.

In fact, when the matter is carefully considered, this truth stands on the very face of the repeated statements of the gospel of John. It is even obvious in the greatest salvation verse of all. For in words most believers know by heart, the apostle quotes our Lord as saying. "For God so loved the world that He gave His only begotten Son, that whoever believes in Him should not perish but have everlasting life" (Jn 3:16).

But here too we meet the very claim that Jesus made to Martha. The Son whom God has given is the One through whom eternal life is found by faith. The believer, therefore, possesses that life and consequently he does not perish.

The message in both passages is precisely the same.

Conclusion

What really happens when a person believes the saving Word of the gospel? There are numerous answers to this question, some of which will be discussed in the pages that follow. But at least two things are so utterly fundamental that they must never be forgotten.

One is that a miraculous new birth occurs within the believer by which one comes into possession of the very life of God.

The other is that the believer knows that he or she has this life.[2]

These two facts make the divine gift every bit as "good and perfect" as James says that God's gifts always are. No one can begin to live a new life until they first receive that life by faith. And no one will be able to live that life effectively who is not sure that it is actually possessed. God's "good and perfect" gift makes provision for both of these basic needs, and they are met at the very moment of faith.

Of course there are people in churches today who have not been born again. But that is our fault and not God's. This is not to be blamed on the fact that God offers salvation freely. Moreover, the problem will not be solved by attaching unbiblical conditions to the message of grace.

Our need is to get out of God's way. We must stop trying to do His work for Him. No amount of stringent lordship teaching will ever accomplish the miracle of new birth. Such teaching, in fact, is an impediment placed in that miracle's path.

What is needed is the simple gospel presented for what it really is—absolutely free! It is this alone which constitutes God's saving Word to the human race. And it is this alone that accomplishes the miracle of regeneration.

5

NO RETURN TRIP

5

No Return Trip

In His encounter with the woman at the well, Jesus made a spectacular promise. He said to her:

Whoever drinks of this water will thirst again, but whoever drinks of the water that I shall give him will never thirst. But the water that I shall give him will become in him a well of water springing up into everlasting life (Jn 4:13–14).

Whatever else she understood from this, the woman of Sychar understood one thing. She understood that Jesus was offering her a drink which would permanently satisfy her thirst. Her response shows this clearly: "Sir, give me this water, that I may not thirst, nor come here to draw" (4.15).

Quite possibly there was now a note of sarcasm in her voice. And it is certain that she does not yet understand the real nature of this offer. Jesus was not talking to her about this well or about the kind of water that was in it.

But at least she had got one thing straight. Whatever this water was, she needed to drink it only once. If it was physical, like the contents of the well before her, she would never have to come back to this well again. There would be no return trip.

And on that point she was exactly right. True, the water Jesus offered her was spiritual and supernatural in character, but the point remained the same. After drinking what He gave, she would never need to come and ask Him for this water again.

It is surprising, however, that this simple reality is often lost from sight in the Christian church. Of course, there are many who directly deny its truth. Instead, they insist, the water of life can be lost through serious disobedience or through departure from the faith. A person who has once possessed it, may need to obtain it again. But, in so saying, they flatly contradict the Lord Himself.

But others do not quite say this. What they do say, in effect, is that the drinking itself must go on and on. And they add that if the drinking ever stops it never really began! But the confusion here is enormous. The simplicity of the Savior's offer is lost sight of completely.

The concept just mentioned is found quite commonly in lordship salvation. According to some of its proponents, if someone "really believes," they will keep on believing to the end of life. And if this supposed faith fails, it was not true faith to begin with.

This view of things is utterly unknown to the Bible. Nevertheless, there are many who have been confused by this kind of teaching. It is necessary, therefore, to look at the Savior's words more closely.

The Forever Gift

The exchange that took place at Sychar's well has as its basic premise the discussion of a gift. According to Jesus, it is one that He would be glad to give the woman upon request (Jn 4:10).

But it is in the nature of gift-giving that, once the gift is bestowed, it is in the possession of the recipient. A single transaction consisting of giving plus receiving suffices to bring the exchange to pass.

That is why the imagery of a drink of water is so pointedly clear in the biblical story. Jesus possesses the water. He gives a drink of it to the Samaritan woman and it is hers forever. Indeed, it transforms her inwardly. From then on she will possess an inward fountain, or "spring," whose supply of water is as unending as eternity itself.

Here again we meet the miracle of regeneration. The life-bearing Word of God accomplishes an inner transformation when it is received in faith. The reception takes place at a point in time—it is like taking a drink of water. But the effects of that drink are unending.

Or to put it another way, the water of life is received *once* and it is possessed *forever*. It is a forever gift!

Naturally, it is not only in the story of the Samaritan woman that we meet this concept. We see it repeatedly in the fourth gospel, both in direct statements and in the images of salvation used by Jesus. For example, in His memorable nighttime conversation with Nicodemus, our Lord said this: "Most assuredly, I say to you, unless one is born again, he cannot see the kingdom of God" (Jn 3:3). This famous declaration deserves the closest consideration.

It is surprising how this conveys the same truth as that found in the totally different image of a drink of water. Birth, too, is a one-time event with permanent consequences. In fact, we have no way at all of reversing our own physical birth.

Even suicide does not really undo it. And although death ends physical life as we currently know it, it does not end our conscious existence at all. Moreover, all who have died will someday know physical experience again (Jn 5:28–29).

By physical birth, therefore, I enter God's creation as an eternal person. I am here forever. There is absolutely nothing I can do about that.

Nor is there anything I can do about regeneration once I have experienced it. By that astonishing miracle I am constituted a child of God. Even if I were to decide I did not want to be His child, it would do me no good. My spiritual birth, like my physical one, is irreversible.

However, it has been suggested that, though I cannot *lose* my salvation, I could *give it back*. But this is ridiculous. I can no more give my spiritual birth back to God than I can give my physical birth back to my earthly parents. If I could, the promises of John's gospel would be proven false. In that case a person who believed in God's Son would perish, contradicting John 3:16. A person who had possessed eternal life would come into judgment, contradicting John 5:24. Or, as we have already observed, a person who drank of Jesus' water would thirst again. But all such experiences are impossible for one who has believed. Jesus Himself said so.

To exactly the same effect are the powerful words recorded in John 5:25. There Jesus says: "Most assuredly, I say to you, the hour is coming, and now is, when the dead will hear the voice of the Son of God; and those who hear will live." Once more we are confronted with an effective image of the miracle of new birth. This time that miracle is compared to resurrection itself.

In the previous verse Jesus has spoken of believers as those who have "passed from death into life" (5:24). How, we might wonder, is so significant a transition accomplished? The answer is found in verse 25. The hour is already here, Jesus affirms, when the spiritually dead are being raised to spiritual life. And the effective instrument in that resurrection is His own voice—His own life-bringing Word.

Obviously here, too, we meet an image that agrees in a marvelous way with the image of new birth or of the single, permanently effective drink. For resurrection is as irreversible as is birth. It is a one-time event with everlasting consequences. That's how it will be for all who are resurrected in the future. Their resurrection will be a single experience whose results will endure for all the ages of eternity.

And that's how it is for all who are raised now by hearing God's saving Word in faith. The results of this resurrection, too, have no end at all.

We are not surprised, therefore, to find the permanence of the saving transaction insisted upon most strongly in John's following chapter. We hear it plainly, for example, in these words: "I am the bread of life. He who comes to Me shall never hunger, and he who believes in Me shall never thirst" (Jn 6:35). "Never hunger"! "Never thirst"! Jesus is saying: "It's permanent! It's permanent!"

But He says it again almost immediately: "All that the Father gives Me will come to Me, and the one who comes to Me I will by no means cast out" (6:37). "By no means cast out." "It's permanent!"

And He says it again:

For I came down from heaven, not to do My own will, but the will of Him who sent Me. And this is the will of the Father who sent Me, that of all He has given Me I should lose nothing, but should raise it up at the last day (Jn 6:38–39).

"Lose *nothing* of all that the Father has given Him!" "Raise it up at the last day!" "It's permanent!"

And yet again: "And this is the will of Him who sent Me, that everyone who sees the Son and believes in Him may have everlasting life; and I will raise him up at the last day" (Jn 6:40).

No wonder that the Savior insisted to Martha that He was both the Resurrection and the Life to every believer. Those things are fully guaranteed. They are part and parcel of the promise that Jesus makes in His offer of salvation. Resurrection will be granted to every believer at the last day. And the believer's experience of God's life, which begins now, will go on throughout the countless ages to follow.

Eternal life, then, is more than just a gift. It is indeed a *forever* gift.

The Forever Appropriation

But from what has just been said, another truth follows unmistakably. If the gift of eternal life is ours forever, then the act of faith which appropriates the gift is definitive and final. This, too, is clear from the images Jesus uses to describe this appropriation.

Let it be recalled again that in speaking to the woman from Sychar our Lord described the exchange He offered in terms of giving and receiving a drink of water. There can be no thought here at all about continuity. The woman was not being asked to drink and drink and drink.[1] She was being asked to drink—once and for all!

Of course this is precisely the contrast with the water in the well on which the Lord Jesus Christ was sitting. Whoever drank from that water would have to drink again and again (Jn 4:13). But not so with the water which Jesus gave (4:14). There would be no drinking of *His* water ever again. The initial drink was sufficient because its results were permanent.

It is just here that we can recognize a serious weakness in much evangelical thought today. In our excessive concentration on the "nature" of faith, we have lost the biblical focus on the gift which faith receives.

After all, taking a drink of water is only a means to an end. It is the water itself that matters, even on the physical level. If the liquid I drink happens to be salt water, it does not matter how skillful or proficient I am at drinking it. Water like that will not satisfy my physical thirst.

But many evangelicals are out of tune with the biblical perspective. In Scripture, saving faith is a simple and uncomplicated issue. We have already discussed this fact in previous chapters.

But the water of life itself is by no means uncomplicated. Indeed, it is totally supernatural. Its effects are marvelous, mysterious, and eternal. Yet the faith that receives so great a gift has the utter directness of childlike trust.

In fact, Jesus Himself insisted, "Assuredly, I say to you, whoever does not receive the kingdom of God as a little child will by no means enter it" (Lk 18:17).

Salvation, therefore, is for those who will receive it in simplicity of heart.

This same straightforward understanding of the saving transaction meets us again in a passage already considered: "Most assuredly, I say to you, the hour is coming, and now is, when the dead will *hear* the voice of the Son of God; and those who *hear* will live" (Jn 5:25; italics added).

With vivid simplicity, our Lord pictures His voice as a mighty power able to penetrate the lifeless ears of those who are spiritually dead. But once it has done so, He declares, the dead are no longer dead. Instead, they have come to life.

Thus, quite obviously, the "hearing" that Jesus is speaking about is nothing less than the believing reception of God's life-giving Word. But once this hearing has occurred, life eternal begins.

It is totally foreign to this imagery to think of anything other than a simple event. God's Word is heard in faith. The result is eternal life.

Naturally, this truth finds a physical illustration in the raising of Lazarus. Lazarus, of course, was very dead indeed!

His sister Martha is reluctant to have the stone removed from the mouth of his tomb because of the stench which would certainly escape from it (Jn 11:39).

But the Lord Jesus Christ, who is the Resurrection and the Life for every believer (Jn 11:25–26), is not hindered by Lazarus's lifeless condition. Instead, with a mere three words—"Lazarus, come forth!"—He penetrated those dead ears and His voice brought this man to life again.

It was as simple as that. The words, "Lazarus, come forth!" (Jn 11:43) were direct, clear, and effective. Lazarus only needed to hear them *once*. From the moment he did, he lived.

And so it is also with the appropriation of God's saving gift to us. It is *one* drink, it is *one* hearing of the Son's voice, that results in the amazing, irreversible miracle of new birth.

How could we possibly have thought of it in any other way?

Accordingly, it is not surprising to discover this very principle in the Bible's greatest discourse on salvation. For, in John 3, when our Lord encountered the inquiring Pharisee named Nicodemus, He made the truth we are talking about unmistakably plain.

In fact, before speaking the lovely words of John 3:16, Jesus said to Nicodemus:

> And as Moses lifted up the serpent in the wilderness, even so must the Son of Man be lifted up, that whoever believes in Him should not perish but have eternal life (Jn 3:14–15).

It would be hard to overstate the value of this pointed prelude to the greatest salvation verse of all.

No one can possibly guess the innumerable people who have found eternal life through John 3:16. Naturally, Jesus knew when He spoke these words that they would bear this kind of abundant fruit. So He introduced them with an extremely effective illustration of salvation.

In doing so, Jesus referred Nicodemus to an Old Testament story found in Numbers 21:4–9.

Here, the children of Israel complained against God and against Moses. As a consequence of this sin, they were attacked by poisonous, fiery serpents, whose bite was fatal.

But when the Israelites begged Moses to pray for them, he did so (Nu 21:7).

Then, acting on the instructions from God, Moses constructed a "bronze serpent, and put it on a pole" (21:9). It was God Himself who told Moses that once he did this "everyone who is bitten, when he looks at it, shall live" (21:8). And that's exactly what happened, so that we read: "And so it was, if a serpent had bitten anyone, when he looked at the bronze serpent, he lived" (Nu 21:9).

What a wonderful and simple visualization of saving faith! As Moses had lifted up the bronze serpent in the desert, so God's Son would be lifted up on the cross of Calvary. Therefore, as God's appointed Savior for sin-stricken humanity, anyone could look to Him in faith and, like the Israelites of old, find life instantaneously.

A single look with eternal life the result. What could be plainer?

But obviously, here too there is no thought of looking and looking and looking. Just as the single drink of living water was an effective appropriation, so too is the single look of faith.

No doubt some modern minds are scandalized by the seeming simplicity of all this.[2] But we need always to remember that we are talking about a divine miracle. And God does not require the stage to be elaborately set for His miraculous activity.

On the contrary! The very simplicity of our responsibility—a single act of trust in Christ—only serves to magnify the miracle God performs. For at the precise instant when a man or woman believes in Christ, at that moment eternity itself invades human experience and transforms our inner beings into something wonderfully and permanently new.

How perfectly the songwriter has captured this truth when he says:

> Born of the Spirit, with life from above
> Into God's fam'ly divine;
> Justified fully through Calvary's love,
> O what a standing is mine!
> And the transaction so quickly was made,
> When as a sinner I came,

Took of the offer of grace He did proffer,
He saved me, O praise His dear name!

Heaven came down and glory filled my soul,
When at the cross the Saviour made me whole;
My sins were washed away
And my night was turned to day—
Heaven came down and glory filled my soul!
          —John W. Peterson
          Heaven Came Down

Let there be no mistake about it. The Bible teaches exactly
that kind of wondrous transaction.

Conclusion

The biblical picture of the saving experience is masterful
in its clarity and simplicity. A single, one-time appropriation
of God's gift results in a miraculous inward transformation
that can never be reversed.

Since this is true, we miss the point to insist that true
saving faith must necessarily continue. Of course, our faith in
Christ *should* continue. But the claim that it absolutely must,
or necessarily does, has no support at all in the Bible. We
will say more about this in subsequent chapters.

For now, however, it is sufficient to observe that the Bible
predicates salvation on an *act* of faith, not on the *continuity*
of faith. Just as surely as regeneration occurs at a point in
time for each individual, so surely does saving faith.

That is why, in the case of Abraham, the moment of his
justification is historically fixed. It is in the precise historical
circumstances described by the context of Genesis 15 that
we read: "And he believed in the Lord, and He accounted it
to him for righteousness" (Ge 15:6).

So, according to the biblical record, it was on this
occasion—and on this occasion only—that Abraham was
justified by faith. The statement of Genesis 15:6 is utterly
unique in the scriptural account. Nothing like it is to be
found anywhere else in the inspired narrative of the patri-
arch's life.

Nor should we expect there to be. After all, both justification and new birth are unrepeatable events, just as is the

faith that appropriates them. Both events occur at the same point in time for every Christian, and that particular historical moment is also the moment of saving faith.

Through justification we acquire the very *righteousness* of God, which is credited to us on the basis of faith alone (Ro 3:21, 22). Through regeneration we acquire the very *life* of God, which is imparted to us likewise on the basis of faith alone. Therefore, in a moment of time we obtain both perfect acceptance before the bar of God's justice as well as full membership in His family.

And all of this is absolutely free and absolutely permanent. "For the gifts and the calling of God are irrevocable" (Ro 11:29).

There is no return trip.

6

SCHOOL DAYS

6

School Days

Few words that Jesus spoke are more profound or challenging than those on the subject of discipleship which He delivered one day to the multitudes. According to Luke, our Lord said the following to these crowds: "If any one comes to Me and does not hate his father and mother, wife and children, brothers and sisters, yes, and his own life also, he cannot be My disciple" (Lk 14:26).

Of course, Jesus was a traveling rabbi—an itinerant teacher. The ancient Greco-Roman world was quite familiar with this type of person. Even outside of Palestine, specialists in philosophy, or rhetoric, or some other branch of knowledge, traveled from place to place earning their livelihood from the information they were able to dispense.

No one expected such instruction to be free. After all, the teacher, or philosopher, had to eat too. So the price of the training he offered was always a relevant question. What would it cost to become his pupil?

That, of course, was exactly what a "disciple" was. The original Greek word meant neither more nor less than a pupil, a learner. The heavy religious overtones which the word "disciple" has today in English did not exist for the multitudes to whom Jesus spoke the words we are discussing.

Of course, Jesus did teach religion, or more precisely, a way of life. But the issue which His words addressed was a simple one: What will my instruction cost you?

Among the multitudes there were undoubtedly many who were deeply impressed by our Lord's public instruction. Some certainly must have been considering whether they wished to become regular pupils of His and to travel with Him to obtain the full benefit of His teaching. What would it be like to be "in school" under this Instructor?

The Lord's answer to their question was startling. "If you don't hate your family," He said, "and even your own life, too, you cannot possibly be My pupil."

It is at once clear that these words set a high price on discipleship. To suggest otherwise is to evade their obvious point.

But equally it should be clear that they have *nothing to do* with the terms on which we receive eternal life. That should not even need saying. Yet, tragically, that does need to be said in the modern church. In fact, it is one of the major errors of lordship theology that it reads the words of Jesus about discipleship as if they were basically no different from the words He spoke to the woman from Sychar about the water of life.[1]

One is tempted to ask, "How can anyone make a mistake like this?" Would not even a child observe that discipleship is obviously hard, while eternal life is free? Can anyone imagine that Luke 14:26 is really saying the same thing as Revelation 22:17, "Whoever desires, let him take the water of life freely"?

Yet lordship thinkers do imagine this and have confused many by teaching it. But no one can understand the New Testament who does not see the obvious difference between the gift of life and being a pupil of Jesus Christ.

Indeed, to ignore this vital distinction is to invite confusion and doctrinal error of the worst kind. For that reason we must look at this fundamental difference with the most careful attention.

Growing Up

An earthly father, who has just taken his newborn son into his arms, does not need to be told that his boy is alive. He is joyfully aware of that fact.

But he is also aware that his son can do absolutely nothing for himself. The infant he holds is simply a bundle of life filled with unrealized capacity. A lot of nurture and training lie ahead.

Not only that, but the worldly experience into which this child has entered is beset with difficulties and dangers. Among these are the threats of disease, disability, and external harm. Growing up well should never be taken for granted.

Nor does the Bible take spiritual growth for granted. The fact is that God's Word is unmistakably clear about the hazards that stand in the way of spiritual development. That is why the most famous of our Lord's pupils, Peter himself, wrote these words: "Therefore, laying aside all malice, all guile, hypocrisy, envy, and all evil speaking, as newborn babes, desire the pure milk of the word, that you may grow thereby" (1Pe 2:1–2).

Certain traits, says the apostle, are harmful to a Christian's "health," and one ingredient in particular is essential to it. Among the poisons to be avoided are malice, deceit, pretense, envy, and slander. Indispensable nourishment, however, is found in the milk of God's Word. But poison mixed with milk can be lethal.

Today there exists in part of the evangelical church a wholly unrealistic view of the nature of Christian experience. According to those who hold this view, effective Christian living is virtually an inevitable result of new birth. But this view is as remote from the Bible as east is remote from west.

Of course, it is a miraculous truth that at the moment of new birth, the very life of God is imparted to the believer. But like the impartation of physical life itself, spiritual life is not granted in fully developed form. It does not come to us in a prefabricated condition.

On the contrary, regeneration brings with it immense capacities and staggering possibilities. But all these capabilities come, so to speak, not in their ripened maturity, but in the form of a "seed" which requires cultivation.

Again, it is Peter who confirms this concept, for he describes his readers as "having been born again, not of corruptible seed but incorruptible, through the word of God which lives and abides forever" (1Pe 1:23).

It follows, therefore, that Christian experience can appropriately be described, with Peter, as a process of growth. But equally it can also be described as a process of education. Indeed, in the original language, Peter's phrase, "the pure milk of the Word" (1Pe 2:2), uses a term that suggests that this "milk" is connected with the mental and rational aspects of man's experience. It is thus an *educating* Word.[2]

No responsible earthly parent thinks that the growth and education of his child are automatic in a world where even physical development can be stunted and where mental and psychological development are even more at risk. Such a view of physical life would be extremely naive.

In the same way, the Bible encourages hard-headed realism about the problems confronting the growth of spiritual experience in a world wracked by sin. Not the least of the barriers to this kind of experience is the physical body into which God's life has been placed. That is why Paul, in a statement that is very much neglected, can write these words: "And if Christ is in you, *the body is dead* because of sin, but the Spirit is life because of righteousness" (Ro 8:10; italics added).

Let it be noted that this is a description of a Christian, one in whom Christ and the Spirit live. Yet the physical house which contains them is spiritually dead!

No wonder that Paul thus conceives of two possible kinds of experience for the believer—one dictated by the body in its deadness, or one dictated by life in the Spirit of Christ. The two options are clearly spelled out by the apostle: "For if you live according to the flesh you will die; but if you through the Spirit put to death the deeds of the body, you will live" (Ro 8:13).

This assertion is every bit as simple as it sounds. Pursue sin, warns Paul, and your experience will be an experience that accords with the deadness of your physical body.[3] Put sin to death, however, and your experience will be that of the living Spirit within you.

Of course, Paul knew something about the intense struggle these options could generate, as his description of that struggle shows so graphically in Romans 7:15–25. The basic truth is expressed in the final verse:

> So then, with the mind I myself serve [as a slave] the law of God, but with the flesh [I serve as a slave] the law of sin (Ro 7:25; the bracketed words are implied by the form and language of the text).

Naturally, only a regenerate person has an inward nature *enslaved,* so to speak, to the law of God. Only one who is born again can truly "delight in the law of God according to the inward man" (Ro 7:22).

By contrast, an unregenerate person is dead in trespasses and sins, has his understanding darkened, and is alienated from the life of God by ignorance and hardness of heart (Eph 2:1; 4:18). Paul's words in Romans 7 cannot possibly describe such an individual.

What they do describe is the astounding enigma of Christian experience. The believer in Jesus is alive in spirit, while still inhabiting a physical house which is as dead to God's life as it can possibly be.

No wonder Paul cries out: "O wretched man that I am! Who will deliver me from this body of death" (Ro 7:24)?

No wonder, too, that new birth needs to be followed immediately by spiritual education!

The Cost of Education

Every human being possesses physical life as a parental gift, just as every Christian possesses eternal life as a gift from God, our heavenly Father. But education—in both spheres—requires hard work.

It is only when we deal with the issues of spiritual growth and development, that good works have an appropriate role to play. The Bible is clear that in regard to new birth and justification they have no role at all.

The apostle Paul, in particular, exhausts the resources of language to make this point clear. Thus, in Romans 4, he writes: "Now to him who works, the wages are not counted as grace but as debt" (Ro 4:4). If works are involved, Paul declares, the payoff is not a product of grace at all. The wages are earned!

Nor is this view an unguarded slip on Paul's part. He says it again elsewhere: "And if by grace, then it is no longer of works; otherwise grace is no longer grace. But if it is of works, then it is no longer grace; otherwise work is no longer work" (Ro 11:6).

This, too, is very clear. Nothing can be by grace and by works at the same time. They are mutually exclusive. To mix them is to alter in a radical way their character. Either grace would cease to be grace, or works would cease to be works. Paul's text plainly says this.[4]

By contrast, lordship theology sometimes evades this truth by claiming that Paul only contrasts grace with self-righteous works or works wrought to achieve merit before God.[5] But this distinction is without foundation in Pauline thought. The apostle speaks here, and elsewhere, simply of works.[6] If God accepts us by grace it cannot have anything to do with works of any kind.

When, therefore, lordship teachers claim that "salvation is a gift, yet it costs everything,"[7] they are not speaking the language of the Bible.

The language that the Bible does speak is plain for all willing to hear: "But to him who *does not work* but believes on Him who *justifies* the ungodly, his faith is counted for righteousness" (Ro 4:5; italics added).

This principle, applied here to justification, is precisely the same for regeneration as well:

> *Not by works of righteousness* which we have done, but according to His mercy He saved us, by *the washing of regeneration* and renewing of the Holy Spirit, whom He poured out on us abundantly through Jesus Christ our Savior, that having been *justified by His grace* we should become heirs according to the hope of *eternal life* (Tit 3:5–7; italics added).

And who could forget the marvelous declaration found in the second chapter of Paul's epistle to the Ephesians? In that famous text he says: "For by grace you have been saved through faith, and that not of yourselves; it is the gift of God, not of works, lest anyone should boast" (Eph 2:8, 9). Paul assures us that works play no role whatsoever in salvation. The saving experience is by grace through faith alone. It is God's free gift to us.

Yet works do have a role in the Christian's experience *after* spiritual birth and justification. In the passage cited above, Paul goes on to say so: "For we are His workmanship, created in Christ Jesus for good works, which God has prepared beforehand that we should walk in them" (Eph 2:10).

Sometimes this text is misunderstood. Sometimes it is read as though it meant that the believer will most certainly walk in the good works God has prepared for him. *But Paul does not say that at all.*

Instead, Paul declares God's *purpose* for us. God *wants* us to walk in good works. Whether we do so or not depends on the many biblical factors which are relevant to spiritual development.

A comparable text is found in John 3:17: "For God did not send His Son into the world to condemn the world, but that the world through Him might be saved." Once again, this passage does not assert that the world *will* be saved. Rather it asserts that God *wants* it to be and that He sent His Son to make this possible.

After all, God "desires all men to be saved and to come to the knowledge of the truth" (1Ti 2:4). But what God *desires* to come to pass, and what in His wisdom He *decrees* will come to pass, are not always the same thing.

Let it be stated plainly. The Greek phrase in Ephesians 2:10 ("that we should walk in them") is exactly the same kind of phrase as is found in John 3:17 ("that the world through Him might be saved"). In neither text do we find that there is any kind of guarantee that the stated purpose will be fulfilled.

The sending of God's Son, therefore, made ample provision for the world to escape divine condemnation and to be saved. But it did not guarantee this. In this same way, God's miracle of salvation in our lives, accomplished by grace through faith without works, makes ample provision for the lifetime of good works for which He has designed us. But it does not guarantee this.

Nevertheless, by this gracious miracle we have become God's workmanship. And since He is a Master Artisan, no two products of His workmanship are exactly alike. Each of us, therefore, is His special creation in Christ Jesus. And for each of us are prepared special and particular works which we are perfectly designed to accomplish.

But accomplishing them requires effort on our part.

This is precisely what the apostle Peter teaches us in his second epistle. First, he declares the ample provisions which God has made for us in the saving experience. God, he affirms, "has given to us all things that pertain to life and godliness, through the knowledge of Him who has called us by glory and virtue" (2Pe 1:3). But this is not an invitation to passivity. On the contrary, it is a call to diligence:

> But also for this very reason, *giving all diligence*, add to your faith virtue, to virtue knowledge, to knowedge self-control, to self-control perseverance, to perseverance godliness, to godliness brotherly kindness, and to brotherly kindness love. *For if these things are yours* and abound, they keep you from being *either barren or unfruitful* in the knowledge of our Lord Jesus Christ (2Pe 1:5–8; italics added).

The Christian experience, therefore, begins with faith. By faith we appropriate God's gift of life with all its matchless potentials. That much is absolutely free.

But from there on there must be diligence. There has to be a willingness to work, and to work hard. To be sure, God will generously give His help as we do so. But we must *want* that help, we must *reach out* for it, we must *be willing* to apply all perseverance to the process of Christian growth. There is no other way to fruitfulness.

A spiritual education is indeed available to us. But to get it, we must be willing to pay the price.

Conclusion

In a classic Pauline text on spiritual education, the apostle writes as follows:

> For the grace of God that brings salvation has appeared to all men, *teaching us* that, denying ungodliness and worldly lusts, we should live soberly, righteously, and godly in the present age (Tit 2:11–12; italics added).

The original word Paul uses here for "teaching" is a word especially applied in Greek usage to the education and training of a child. The message of God's saving grace is for "all men," but the education it brings is for "us," God's born-again children.

But Paul was very far from assuming that the educational process would inevitably be effective for all believers. As he demonstrates everywhere in his epistles, he was a down-to-earth realist about the spiritual dangers that confronted his converts, and about the possibility of failure.

Thus Paul never took good works for granted in the believer's life. Instead, he felt constrained to tell Titus:

> This is a faithful saying, and these things I want you to affirm constantly, that those who have believed in God should be careful to maintain good works. These things are good and profitable to men (Tit 3:8).

"Don't let down your guard, Titus," Paul is saying. "Good works are something you constantly need to remind believers about. They have to be extremely careful about maintaining such works, and it is part of your job to see that they are."

So this is the true biblical picture of Christian experience. At our spiritual birth we are lavishly endowed with all the necessary potentials for effective Christian living. But we must be energetic in cultivating these potentials, and if we are producing good works we must be most careful to maintain them.

Or, to put it another way, we need to be fully committed to the goal toward which our spiritual education is leading us. No other goal can be allowed to interfere. Indeed, we must be so dedicated to our Lord that our love for Him excels all other loves. By comparison with our devotion to Him, every secondary love must seem like hatred.

"That's what it will cost you to be my pupil," Jesus was saying to the crowds (Lk 14:26). "My curriculum is so demanding that it is not possible for you to be my student without 'hating' your father and mother, wife and children, brothers and sisters and, yes, even your very own life."

"Before you enroll, think about it!"

7

DROPPING OUT

7

Dropping Out

There was a good reason why the Lord Jesus insisted that a person should think carefully about a decision to become His pupil. It was not at all that His curriculum was hard to begin. The problem was that it was difficult to complete.

That is why Jesus spoke as He did immediately after His words about "hating" family and life. For, following the stringent demands He makes in Luke 14:26, He says this:

> And whoever does not bear his cross and come after Me cannot be My disciple. For which of you, intending to build a tower, does not sit down first and count the cost, whether he has enough to finish it . . . (Lk 14:27–28).

It is not a falsely glamorous picture that the Son of God paints here of discipleship. If someone wished to follow Him as his Teacher, there was a burden to be carried along the road. That burden is described as a cross.

No doubt it was only later, in the afterlight of the events of Calvary, that the church fully understood the impact of this statement. But even for the multitudes who first heard it, it must have sounded solemn enough.

Criminals were crucified on such pieces of wood. Most of Jesus' hearers had probably witnessed a crucifixion. The overtones of the word "cross" were ominous. What might that mean for a pupil of this Teacher?

Whatever it meant, the hearer could at least sense the appropriateness of our Lord's next statement. There was a cost involved in becoming His disciple, just as there was a cost involved in building a tower. No sensible builder would start to erect a tower (though some foolish ones had done so) without calculating whether he could afford to see it through to completion. Any failure to make this preliminary reckoning could lead to considerable embarrassment later.

Thus Jesus went on to say, ". . . lest, after he has laid the foundation, and is not able to finish it, all who see it begin to mock him, saying, 'This man began to build and was not able to finish'" (14:29, 30).

"It is possible," Jesus is saying, "that you might start out as a 'pupil' of mine, but that you might not be able to stay the course. You may not be able to finish."

Unfortunately, many Christian teachers do not possess the frankness that Jesus Himself displayed on the subject of discipleship. They are not very candid in warning believers that the educational process can be hard, and that "dropping out" of it is a danger that must be faced frankly.

The simple fact is that the New Testament never takes for granted that believers will see discipleship through to the end. And it never makes this kind of perseverance either a condition or a proof of final salvation from hell.

What it does do, repeatedly, is to warn believers about the danger of *not* persevering. To put it in modern terms, the Bible warns Christians against "dropping out" of the educational process.

The Challenge to Go On

No sensible earthly parents would assume that their child will finish school simply because the child is theirs. Even in highly literate families, where the chances are good that all the children will complete their education, it may actually happen that one or more of them will not.

The possible reasons for this are legion. A learning impairment may prevent a child from finishing his schooling. The lure of drugs (so prevalent now that even younger children are at risk) can be another reason. Or there may be psychological problems, physical disease, or social maladjustment.

The realistic parent is aware of all these dangers and takes nothing for granted. Whenever necessary, the parent will urge the child to avoid pitfalls and to persevere in the educational experience.

But God the Father does exactly the same thing. Where did we ever get the idea that He does not?

Indeed, in a truly lovely passage in the book of Hebrews, the anonymous author issues a ringing challenge to persevere in the Christian pathway. But before doing this, he summarizes the spiritual privilege of access to God, which his Christian readers possessed. He writes:

> Therefore, brethren, having boldness to enter the Holiest by the blood of Jesus, by a new and living way which He has consecrated for us, through the curtain, that is, His flesh, and having a High Priest over the house of God, let us draw near with a true heart in full assurance of faith, having our hearts sprinkled from an evil conscience and our bodies washed with pure water (Heb 10:19–22).

This memorable and exquisite expression of Christian privilege is rightly treasured by many. But, clearly, those to whom the author speaks are Christians. And to these Christians the writer at once expresses a genuine concern:

> Let us *hold fast* the confession of our hope without wavering, for He who promised is faithful. And let us consider one another in order to stir up love and good works, *not forsaking the assembling of ourselves together*, as is the manner of some, but exhorting one another, and so much the more as you see the Day approaching (10:23–25; italics added).

"Be careful," warns this writer, "that you don't drop out of school. Hold fast to your Christian hope."

Naturally, the church itself was an indispensable spiritual classroom where so much of God's truth was learned by such early believers as these. To give up gathering with other believers for instruction and worship, and even to abandon one's Christian confession, was nothing less than surrendering one's status as a pupil—a disciple—of Jesus Christ.

Of course, there are those who try to divert this warning to merely professing Christians who are not actually Christians at all. If that is what the writer of Hebrews really thought, he has done a superb job of concealing it!

Let the reader of our book look again at the verses just quoted from this great epistle (Heb 10:19–25). Apart from pure theological prejudice, who would ever suspect that the warning here was not intended for real Christians?

The same thing is true of the writer's words later in the chapter:

> But recall the former days in which, after you were illuminated, you endured a great struggle with sufferings: . . . for you had compassion on me in my chains, and joyfully accepted the plundering of your goods, knowing in yourselves that you have a better and an enduring possession in heaven (Heb 10:32, 34).

Once more the readers are regarded as Christians—and as Christians who know that they have possessions in heaven.

But immediately the writer adds: "Therefore do not cast away your confidence, which has great reward" (10:35). "Hold on! Hold on!" says the author. "Don't throw away the confidence that is leading you to a great reward!"[1]

It follows, therefore, that it is simply a theological illusion to maintain that a Christian who has embarked on the pathway of discipleship could never abandon it. In the spiritual realm, this notion is as naive as an earthly father who declares, "*My* son would never drop out of school!"

It is thus profoundly significant that Paul compares the Christian life to a racecourse in which winning is not automatic for any runner, not even for himself. Specifically he writes:

> Do you not know that those who run in a race [or, stadium] all run, but one receives the prize? Run in such a way that you may obtain it . . . Therefore I run thus: not with uncertainty. Thus I fight: not as one who beats the air. But I discipline my body and bring it into subjection, *lest, when I have preached to others, I myself should become disqualified* (1Co 9:24, 26–27; italics added).

"Not even I take winning this race for granted," Paul declares. "Instead, I do all that I can to avoid being disqualified at the end."

Again, there is no thought here of the loss of eternal life. Such a loss is impossible, as our Lord Himself made clear.[2] But the apostle can indeed envision the possibility that even he—a preacher to others—might lose the reward that God grants to successful runners.

It was only when Paul stood at the threshold of martyrdom that he could survey his entire Christian life with a rich sense of victory. His words are justly famous:

> I have fought the good fight, I have finished the race, I have kept the faith. Finally, there is laid up for me the crown of righteousness, which the Lord, the righteous Judge, will give me on that Day, and not to me only, but also to all who have loved His appearing (2Ti 4:7–8).

No Christian life can be pronounced a success unless it *ends* successfully. The race is not over simply because we have been running it for years. Or to put it another way, the task of constructing the tower of Christian discipleship calls for firm perseverance until that tower is finished (Lk 14:28). To quit is to invite mockery from the world around us, and to bring disgrace to the name of our Lord.

But if anyone supposes that no true Christian could quit, or would quit, they have not been paying attention to the Bible. They need to reread their New Testament. This time, with their eyes open.

Warning the Lost

One thing is obvious from what has been said so far. If the educational process called discipleship is so demanding, no one should try to enroll in it who does not yet possess the spiritual capacities that are freely given at the moment of new birth.

But some do make this attempt. Consequently, in addressing the multitudes about the demands of discipleship to Himself, our Lord must certainly have had this fact in mind.

Of course, as has already been pointed out, Jesus wants *any* prospective pupil of His to weigh His demands most carefully. This is not only evident from what He says about building a tower, but also from His words which follow. Just as surely as the Lord counsels a would-be pupil to "sit down," like a tower builder, "and count the cost," so He also says:

> Or what king, going to make war against another king, does not sit down first and consider whether he is able with ten thousand to meet him who comes against him with twenty thousand? Or else, while the other is still a great way off, he sends a delegation and asks conditions of peace (Lk 14:31-32).

"Becoming My pupil," says Jesus, "is like going to war. Moreover, it is like going to war against forces which greatly outnumber you. It is foolish to rush into battle without considering whether the battle can be won."

Naturally, even born-again Christians need to hear this kind of sobering assessment. Discipleship to Jesus Christ is not an invitation to a Sunday school picnic. It is an invitation to spiritual warfare.

Nevertheless, a Christian has the resources for this battle by virtue of regeneration. So, with reliance upon God and with wholehearted commitment to Christ, he or she can look forward to the kind of victory that the apostle Paul achieved. In the strength which God will generously supply, the believer can indeed fight the good fight and finish the race.

But how can the unsaved do that? Of course, they cannot. They have no chance at all of finishing well. They need to hear our Lord's warning most urgently.

Yet, the fact still remains that despite such stern words as these, unsaved men did attach themselves to Jesus while He was still on earth. To put it simply, there were unregenerate people who enrolled as His pupils.

Judas is the classic example of this, but there were others. This fact is made plain to us by the Lord Himself in an important passage found in the gospel of John.

On one occasion, after the Savior had spoken His discourse on the bread of life, His disciples are thrown into turmoil. They are particularly upset by our Lord's illustration of saving faith as an appropriation of Himself in His incarnate humanity. He describes this appropriation as the act of eating His flesh and drinking His blood (Jn 6:53–58). Confusion swiftly follows in the ranks of His pupils:

"'Therefore many of His disciples, when they heard this, said, 'This is a hard saying; who can understand it?'" (Jn 6:60).

In reply, Jesus warns these disciples that their confusion about His words leaves them unprepared for more difficult truth which lies ahead (Jn 6:61–62). If truth related to His incarnation offends them, how much more will truth related to His return to glory offend them? Moreover, He says, they have taken His words too literally, rather than in the spiritual sense in which they were intended (6:63). Thereupon, He adds: "But there are some of you who do not believe" (Jn 6:64a).

No wonder some of them had problems with our Lord's imagery about the act of saving faith. They did not have such faith for they had never appropriated Him as the Bread of Life.

But let us note one thing carefully. John the Evangelist writes that "*many* of His disciples" found His words difficult (6:60). Yet Jesus says, "*Some* of you" do not believe (6:64).

Confusion did not necessarily arise in the minds of only unregenerate disciples. Regenerate disciples might also be puzzled by this rich, new image of the saving act of appropriation. But at least *some* of the confused were unsaved. This was no surprise to Jesus at all: "For Jesus knew from the beginning who they were who did not believe, and who would betray Him" (Jn 6:64b).

But if He knew, why had He let them start out on the pathway of discipleship in the first place? Is not the answer completely obvious? He *loved* them—even Judas. Moreover, "the Son of Man" had "come to seek and to save that which was lost" (Lk 19:10). If they wanted to sit under His teaching day after day, why not let them? That way He could *seek them* day after day.

After all, the Bible declares that "God our Savior . . . desires all men to be saved and to come to the knowledge of the truth" (1Ti 2:3–4). His love is boundless and is directed toward every man.

Frequently (though not always) lordship salvation is combined with a harsh system of thought that denies the reality of God's love for every single human being. According to this kind of theology, God dooms most men to eternal damnation long before they are born and really gives His Son to die only for the elect.[3]

For such thinkers, the declaration that "God so loved the world" (Jn 3:16) must be tortured into meaning something less than His universal love for humankind. It does not lie within the scope of this book to deal with this tragic error. The author can only trust that most readers will be content to rest on the simple assertions of Scripture about God's feelings and provision for lost people (Jn 1:7, 29; 3:16–17; 4:42; 12:32; 2Co 5:19; 1Ti 2:1–6; 4:10; Tit 2:11; 2Pe 3:9; 1Jn 2:2).

No one denies that there is an element of mystery about the way in which God's sovereign purposes relate to our own responsibility to choose what is good and right. The Bible does not seek to resolve this tension for us any more than it seeks to unravel the mystery of the Trinity.

No system of thought which reduces human beings to mere robots, or to a collection of puppets on strings, does justice to the Bible's deep insistence on human responsibility. For our current purposes, we assume that God is truly sovereign and accomplishes all the ends He decrees. But we also assume that each individual is genuinely responsible to respond to the goodness of God, our Creator. Many texts make this plain (e.g., Ro 1:18–21; Ac 14:14–17; 17:24–29). And where there is a real search for God, He rewards it (Heb 11:6).

So it was really an act of goodness and love for Jesus to allow unsaved disciples to travel with Him. He thereby enhanced their opportunity to come to saving faith in Himself. But at the same time, this very privilege deepened their responsibility before God if they did not.

Perhaps some of these unsaved disciples did eventually appropriate the Bread of Life. Judas, of course, never did so. But in thinking of the others, we do not know. The Bible does not say.

What the Bible does say is that, on this occasion, many of His pupils "dropped out": "From that time many of His disciples went back and walked with Him no more" (Jn 6:66).

Again, we must be careful. Jesus said *some* did not believe; John says *many* left Him. There is no reason to think that all of those who left were unsaved. In fact, there is reason to suspect the opposite. For what we read next is this: "Then Jesus said to the twelve, 'Do you also want to go away?'" (Jn 6:67). "Are you committed?" Jesus asks. "Let me hear you say so." Clearly, His words imply, "It is not impossible for you men to leave too."

But what we must note especially is our Lord's directness with His unsaved pupils. Their position was precarious indeed. Despite the stern terms which Jesus had publicly laid down for discipleship, they enrolled anyway. Yet no happy end was possible for them, unless they believed in Him for eternal life. So He told them in frank words, "Some of you haven't done that yet."

Here there is no confusion between discipleship and salvation, as there is today in lordship theology. On the one hand, it is never taken for granted that discipleship will be successfully pursued to the end even by the saved. On the other hand, it is recognized that someone could correctly be described as a disciple who is not yet even born again.

Thus our Lord's public warnings about the demands imposed by His course of instruction are doubly appropriate. Anyone at all who might be inclined to enroll should consider this decision with the utmost care!

Conclusion

Discipleship to the Lord Jesus Christ obviously is intended for those who have been regenerated through faith in Him. But discipleship—even today—involves public preaching and teaching. We should not be surprised if unsaved people are sometimes drawn into this process. Indeed, they even join churches.

We cannot always tell when this has happened, however, as our omniscient Lord could tell. But we can learn from His example. We need always to keep the issue of the gospel separate and distinct from the process of spiritual education. We should not assume that a man or woman is born again just because they are found in the ranks of Christian disciples.

Our preaching and teaching should always make clear that discipleship does not save.

Indeed, discipleship is neither a condition nor a proof of actual regeneration. Only faith in Christ for eternal life produces genuine new birth. No one who sits under our teaching and preaching should be led to think in any other way.

But, on the other hand, we certainly must not assume that a person who has "dropped out" of the process is necessarily *un*saved. They may in fact have found their spiritual education more taxing than expected; they may have failed to count the cost correctly.

No one who heard Jesus teach in public could be under the impression that being His pupil was easy or inexpensive. His warnings were unmistakable on this point. Education under Him was extremely demanding, and He said so.

And so should we. Indeed, it is our responsibility to make the issues clear: Salvation is absolutely free; discipleship most certainly is not.

8

THE ROYAL BATTLE

8

The Royal Battle

Nothing that Jesus ever said was said carelessly. His pupils down through the centuries have realized this fact. They have learned that everything their Teacher ever taught requires repeated and close attention.

That is certainly true of the words Jesus spoke comparing discipleship to warfare. Let us consider those words again:

> Or what king, going to make war against another king, does not sit down first and consider whether he is able with ten thousand to meet him who comes against him with twenty thousand? (Lk 14:31).

The contents of this statement are quite striking. "Being my pupil," declares Jesus, "is like being a king who is at war with another king. Moreover, the enemy king looks over-whelmingly powerful."

"Discipleship," the Lord is saying, "is a royal battle. It is a conflict between two kings."

With the rest of the New Testament at hand, the meaning of this becomes clear. The believer in Jesus Christ is a royal person, the regenerate child of the King Eternal. Moreover, the believer holds membership in a "royal priesthood" (1Pe 2:9). Beyond that, if one perseveres in the Christian pathway, kingly power is promised. For, "if we endure, we shall also reign with Him" (2Ti 2:12).

But the other king is easily identified too. He can be none other than "the ruler of this world" (Jn 14:30), "the prince of the power of the air, the spirit who now works in the sons of disobedience" (Eph 2:2). He is indeed "the god of this age" who "has blinded the minds of those who do not believe" (2Co 4:4). He is Satan himself.

Obviously, then, this king is well endowed with forces. Not only does he blind the minds of unbelieving men whom he can then manipulate, but he is also in command of powerful spiritual hosts who operate under his command.

The apostle Paul speaks graphically of these supernatural enemies of ours. In so doing, he also describes the Christian life as a warfare. His words are both sobering and inspirational:

> For we do not wrestle against flesh and blood, but against principalities, against powers, against the rulers of the darkness of this age, against spiritual wickedness in the heavenly places. Therefore take up the whole armor of God, that you may be able to withstand in the evil day, and having done all, to stand (Eph 6:12–13).

The battle is real, according to Paul, and in our conflict we are locked in a struggle with opponents whose capacities and strengths far exceed our own. Yet victory is possible, if we avail ourselves of the resources God places at our disposal.

But we must wear the armor He provides. If we don't, we invite swift defeat.

No wonder Jesus challenged would-be pupils of His to consider the education He offered as a form of conflict. An enemy king—Satan himself—would most certainly come against them with all of the forces he could muster. It would be unfair not to make this plain.

But in lordship salvation these things are not made plain at all. Instead, they are sadly obscured.

According to lordship theology, the failure to persevere successfully in the Christian race and in the Christian warfare is a sign that one is not really born again. All true Christians end up as winners, we are told. All true Christians end up as conquerors. But if losing and defeat are not possibilities for the Christian, then the race and the battle are not real.

In fact this point of view is a ready formula for defeat. It is even a kind of unilateral spiritual disarmament. Its consequences are extremely grave, playing beautifully into the hands of our enemy.

These profound issues must be carefully considered.

Spiritual Morale

Every effective military leader knows that troop morale is a vital element if victory is to be achieved. If the forces under his command are discouraged and demoralized, defeat is a likely prospect.

What lordship salvation really does is to strike a heavy blow to Christian morale. Instead of assuring that the believer belongs to God, come what may, lordship teachers tell Christians that they should actually verify their salvation by victorious living. If one is really saved, this will be proved by the way he defeats the enemy. After all, *real* Christians are winners.

And if the believer loses? Well, that can occur at times, but "losing" must not take place too often or last too long. Within the framework of lordship thought, if one suffers a serious or prolonged spiritual defeat, then their salvation might well be called into question. The heart of the matter, then, for lordship doctrine, is that my very identity as a Christian hangs on how well I fight.

This is a little like telling soldiers to fight hard for their country so that by fighting well they may prove it really is their country! But what soldier will risk life and limb on the battlefield for love of country without being sure to what country he belongs?

Of course, a mercenary soldier might take great risks if the purse was rich enough. In ancient times there were many such hired combatants, who fought for money alone. But if a soldier fights only for compensation there are obvious limits to his loyalty.

Lordship teaching essentially makes mercenary soldiers out of Christians. From the lordship perspective Christians will only fight vigorously if the stakes are great enough. And what stakes could be greater than heaven or hell? Thus the battle is turned into a test of one's salvation.

Christian soldiers are not mercenaries however. They do not fight to prove their salvation, much less to win it. They know that they are citizens of heaven, and this assurance is a powerful motivation in battle. Indeed, one of the most overlooked aspects of New Testament teaching is the extent to which the writers appeal to their readers' assurance of salvation. They use this assurance as an effective motivational tool in exhorting believers to spiritual victory.

A classic example of such motivation was penned by the apostle Paul in his first letter to the Corinthians. He is discussing the problem of sexual immorality, which was very pervasive in the city of Corinth. He writes: "Do you not know that your bodies are members of Christ? Shall I then take the members of Christ and make them members of a harlot? Certainly not!" (1Co 6:15).

"Aren't you aware," says Paul, "that as Christians your physical bodies are in union with Christ?" In Greek, the form of this question implied that he expected an affirmative response. But it should be noted as well that the question does *not* ask, "Don't you know you are saved?" Instead it asks, "Don't you know what your salvation implies?"

As Christians, Paul is arguing, we should understand that our physical bodies are spiritually joined to Christ and thus we ought to take care not to use them in an immoral way.

A few verses later the apostle also says this:

> Flee sexual immorality. Every sin that a man does is outside the body, but he who commits sexual immorality sins against his own body. Or do you not know that your body is the temple of the Holy Spirit *who is in you, whom you have from God, and you are not your own? For you were bought at a price;* therefore glorify God in your body and in your spirit, *which are God's* (1Co 6:18–20; italics added).

How different this is from the spirit of lordship salvation. Paul does not say, as lordship teachers so often do, that his readers should question their salvation if they become involved in sexual impurity.

On the contrary, Paul appeals to the fact that they are saved as a primary reason why they should "flee sexual immorality." He urges them to focus on the sacredness of their physical bodies as temples of the Holy Spirit. He points them to the price by which they became God's property. He insists that their conduct should be motivated by the reality of their relationship to the Lord!

It is precisely the power of such an appeal that is lost in lordship thought. Deep down inside, lordship teachers believe that a fear of judgment motivates more effectively than grace. They are more at home with legalistic threatenings about hell than with the power of God's unconditional love in Christ.

So far are the lordship teachers out of tune with the New Testament that they actually feel that if assurance is not conditioned on good works, a person is more likely to sin!

But the error in this is transparent. When God gives a person the water of life absolutely free, that water becomes "in him a well of water springing up into everlasting life" (Jn 4:14). A moral appeal based on the realization that God's life is within us thus becomes the most powerful moral appeal that can possibly be made. It is nothing less than an appeal to the supernatural reality of that inward fountain of life. It is an appeal to our deepest spiritual instincts.

Thus all the thunderings and lightnings from Mt. Sinai cannot be compared for a moment in motivational power to the "still, small voice" of God's gracious love to us in Christ, which comes through Mt. Calvary.

Be What You Are

We must say it again. The New Testament authors repeatedly base their exhortations to holy living on the readers' knowledge and assurance of God's saving grace. In a sense they tell Christians over and over again, "Be what you are!" Or to put it another way: "Since you are Christians, live as Christians should live."

It is not possible in a book like this to exhaust the examples of this kind of admonition. But a few more instances should be noted in order to emphasize this crucial point. Readers will find many more examples upon examining the New Testament.

In exhorting the Thessalonians not to be caught unaware

by the advent of the Day of the Lord, Paul writes these
words:

> But you, brethren, are not in darkness, that this Day should
> overtake you as a thief. *You are all sons of light and sons of
> the day.* We are not of the night nor of darkness. Therefore, let
> us not sleep, as others do, but let us watch and be sober (1Th
> 5:4–6; italics added).

This passage hardly needs comment. "Don't be unwatchful,
as unsaved people are," writes the apostle, "because you *all*
belong to the day and are sons of light." "Be what you are,"
says Paul.

Again the apostle writes: "For you were once darkness,
but now you are light in the Lord. Walk as children of light"
(Eph 5:8).

"Be what you are," Paul says.

To the same effect is an earlier statement in the same
epistle: "And be kind to one another, tenderhearted, forgiving one another, just as God in Christ also has forgiven you"
(Eph 4:32). "You have been forgiven," Paul is saying. "So
now be forgiving toward others."

In a particularly exquisite passage, the apostle puts it this
way:

> For our citizenship is in heaven, from which we also eagerly
> wait for the Savior, the Lord Jesus Christ, who will transform
> our lowly body that it may be conformed to His glorious body,
> according to the working by which He is able even to subdue
> all things to Himself. *Therefore,* my beloved and longed-for
> brethren, my joy and crown, *so stand fast* in the Lord, beloved
> (Php 3:20–21 and 4:1; italics added).

What an energizing word this is to Christians on the
battlefield of life! "As citizens of heaven our destiny is to be
gloriously transformed when Christ comes," declares Paul
eloquently. "*Therefore,* stand fast in the Lord."

Obviously, there is nothing here about proving our heavenly citizenship by standing fast. The very reverse is the
case. Precisely because we *are* citizens of heaven we *should*
stand fast. Other New Testament writers share Paul's point
of view. They, too, exhort their readers as people who
already know that they are saved.

We have previously noted how the apostle Peter speaks to his readers about the lavish endowment that was bestowed on them when they came to know Christ. And on the basis of this provision he admonishes them to give "all diligence" to the process of spiritual growth and development (2Pe 1:3–7). But Peter does the same kind of thing in his first epistle as well.

Thus Peter can say:

Therefore gird up the loins of your mind, be sober, and hope to the end for the grace that is to be brought to you at the revelation of Jesus Christ; as obedient children, not conforming yourselves to the former lusts, as in your ignorance; but as He who called you is holy, you also be holy in all your conduct, because it is written, "Be holy, for I am holy" (1Pe 1:13–16).

This is surely a beautiful piece of exhortation. But let it be observed that nothing is assumed here—except that the readers are Christians! They have something to rest in fully as they anticipate the Lord's return. They are God's children, who are now called to holiness. Thus they should not let themselves be conformed to the lifestyle they lived formerly in the days of their unsaved ignorance.

The whole passage moves forward on the shared realization of both the writer and his readers that the readers are genuinely born again. This is even stated directly in 1 Peter 1:22–23. Indeed, exhortation based on the readership's recognition of their own salvation can be found almost anywhere one chooses to examine the New Testament epistles.

This is even found in James, whose lovely letter has suffered much at the hands of interpreters. He writes:

Of His own will He brought us forth by the word of truth, that we might be a kind of firstfruits of His creatures. *Therefore, my beloved brethren,* let every man be swift to hear, slow to speak, slow to wrath; for the wrath of man does not produce the righteousness of God (Jas 1:18–20; italics added).

James makes his point effectively. "We've been born again by the word of truth," he declares. "We are even prototypes for what God will do in all His creation. So I urge you to be eager listeners, but restrained in the tongue and anger."

The rest of the letter suggests that James's readers had need for such admonitions. But regenerate they were. James says so and calls them brethren repeatedly. Neither he nor any other writer of a New Testament epistle ever felt the need to question the Christianity of his readership.[1]

In innumerable ways, therefore, the writers urged their fellow Christians to be "followers of God as dear children" (Eph 5:1), and to live "worthy of the calling with which you were called" (Eph 4:1).

To put it simply, the assurance of salvation is fundamental to all New Testament morality. It is the fixed point of reference out of which Christian obedience must flow.

Conclusion

So that is why lordship theology exposes Christians to spiritual defeat. By stripping us of the unconditional certainty that we possess eternal life, it dangerously erodes the solid ground we need beneath our feet.

To put it another way, by calling the believer's Christian identity into question, lordship theology prevents him or her from drawing from this identity the spiritual strength God intended them to draw. Indeed, such teaching throws the Christian back on legalistic principles whereby one must seek to prove one's relationship to Christ through sustained performance. Gone is the peace that comes from resting in God's grace alone.[2]

Paul did not live that way. Instead, his life proceeded on the basis of deeply held certitudes. He makes this clear to us in a dynamic way:

> For I through the law died to the law that I might live to God. I have been crucified with Christ; it is no longer I who live, but Christ lives in me; and the life which I now live in the flesh I live by faith in the Son of God, who loved me and gave Himself for me (Gal 2:19–20).

But suppose I am not quite sure that I have been crucified with Christ? Suppose I do not know with certainty that

Christ lives in me? How then can I draw upon such wonderful realities, as Paul did, for the life of faith which I must live day by day?

Is it not clear that under lordship teaching every suggestion of spiritual weakness within me, every experience of failure and frustration, can have enormous destructive potential? How soon one will ask: Am I then really saved at all? Do I truly have Christ in me or am I vainly seeking victory in my own unregenerate strength? And in the wake of doubt comes discouragement, despair, and defeat.

Let no one be under any illusions. This is precisely the quagmire into which many have fallen as a result of lordship doctrine. Those who so teach bear a terrible responsibility before God. The spiritual battlefield is littered with their victims.

But it need not be so. For, in discipleship, we move forward as kings to engage the enemy king. We advance precisely because we are the royal offspring of the King of heaven.

And because we *know* it!

9

THE SHIELD OF FAITH

9

The Shield of Faith

Among the vital pieces of spiritual equipment which the believer needs for his conflict with the enemy, the apostle Paul points significantly to "the shield of faith." His well-crafted words are part of his extended description of the Christian's armor in Ephesians 6. There the apostle writes: "Above all, taking the shield of faith with which you will be able to quench all the fiery darts of the wicked one" (Eph 6:16).

Paul's vivid language makes it plain that he is dealing with a crucial item in our spiritual armory. Like the foot soldier of ancient times, the Christian must rely heavily on this piece of equipment when in the thick of the fight.

In fact, the crucial character of the shield is shown by Paul's reference to the flaming arrows of the Devil. It often happened in ancient warfare that foot soldiers came under assault from the archers in the enemies' ranks. As the fusillade of arrows rained down on them, the soldiers could lift their shields above their heads for needed protection. Even flame-tipped arrows could be extinguished as they bounced harmlessly off the shields.

In the same way, Satan's spiritual missiles are aimed at the Christian's most vulnerable points. Their fiery nature, as described by Paul, suggests their capacity not only to wound, but to inflame. Yet the apostle insists that every one of them can be successfully deflected—and extinguished—by "the shield of faith." Clearly, this shield can determine the course of battle.

Would it therefore be surprising if the enemy tried to strike this shield right out of the Christian's hand? Is not such a defensive aid as this sure to become an object of assault by our determined opponent?

Of course it is.

Yet, sadly, the grim reality of Satan's effort to snatch this shield away from us is hardly recognized in lordship salvation teaching. Or, if it is recognized, the Christian is viewed as a virtually impregnable fortress of faith.

It is impossible, so lordship teachers tell us, for the faith of a believer to collapse entirely. The shield of faith can never really be stripped from a Christian's hand, for if the shield is lost, so the logic of this position runs, it was not really a shield at all since the person in question was not a true believer to begin with![1]

Once again, of course, lordship thought is trapped by its unbiblical doctrine of faith. Someone may warmly and sincerely affirm their faith in Christ. Yet if that same person later denies their faith and renounces their convictions, they are said not to have really believed at all.

This is spiritual and psychological nonsense. Every honest person would admit to believing things in the past that are now no longer believed. And everyone also knows that not all the changes in our convictions are changes from error to truth. Sometimes we are wrong about what we now believe.

But these simple, commonsense observations are lost on lordship teachers. God, they say, guarantees the believer's perseverance in the faith. Unfortunately, this dogmatic claim does not have the support of the Bible.[2]

On the contrary, the New Testament is altogether clear that maintaining our faith in God involves a struggle whose outcome is not guaranteed simply by the fact that we are saved. Instead, fighting the good fight of faith is what the spiritual conflict is really all about. To think otherwise is to invite defeat on the spiritual battlefield.

Accordingly, we must look carefully at the testimony of Scripture about this crucial aspect of the Christian's warfare.

Faith Under Attack

One of the most shocking incidents in the entire New Testament is recorded by Luke in the seventh chapter of his gospel, where we read this:

And the disciples of John reported to him concerning all these things. And John, calling two of his disciples to him, sent them to Jesus, saying, "Are You the Coming One, or do we look for another?" When the men had come to Him, they said, "John the Baptist has sent us to You, saying, 'Are You the Coming One, or do we look for another?'" (Lk 7:18–20).

It is hard to believe one's eyes when this passage is first encountered. Here is the great prophet and forerunner of God's Christ calling into question the very Person to whom he had once given bold testimony.

What a contrast Luke's passage is with John's own words recorded in the fourth gospel! For there we are told that the Baptist declared: "Behold! The Lamb of God who takes away the sin of the world!" (Jn 1:29).

Shortly after, John testified this way:

I saw the Spirit descending from heaven like a dove, and He remained upon Him. And I did not know Him, but He who sent me to baptize with water said to me, "Upon whom you see the Spirit descending, and remaining on Him, this is He who baptizes with the Holy Spirit." And I have seen and testified that this is the Son of God (1:32–34).

Yet now John says, through his messengers, "Are You the Coming One, or do we look for another?" The contrast is astounding.

Clearly, then, this great servant of God is asking a question he presumably had settled decisively long ago. His inquiry is manifestly an expression of doubt about the very truth by which men and women are saved. At this point in time, John could not have affirmed with Martha, "Yes, Lord, I believe that You are the Christ, the Son of God, who is to come into the world" (Jn 11:27).

Yet John the Baptist had more reason to believe this truth than most. After all, according to his own testimony, he had seen the Holy Spirit descend like a dove upon our Lord at

His baptism. Moreover, God Himself had informed John that the One upon whom the Spirit descended like that was indeed His Son.

But now the truth God had made so unmistakably clear to him has become an open question for John. Was it really all true, or not?

Our sense of shock over this incident from the Baptist's life is real. Yet at the same time our surprise is unrealistic. Those who have even a superficial grasp on the workings of their own hearts must acknowledge the gripping realism of this part of God's Word.

Doubt can come to us even in the very best of times. But more often it is a side effect of the trials and difficulties of life. One might even describe it as one of the Devil's fiery darts.

John the Baptist had lowered the shield of faith. A flame ignited in his mind and heart, and he burned for some new assurance that his life and ministry were not merely a monumental mistake.

No doubt John's environment made the enemy's attack much easier. In what were surely the dismal conditions of a Herodian prison, beset perhaps also by physical weakness or ill health, John was an inviting target for Satan. That some of the flaming arrows found their mark should surprise no one who is a realist about spiritual warfare.

But let this be said clearly. At the point in his life which Luke describes for us, John the Baptist is *not* believing. On the contrary, he is doubting. And the truth he doubts is nothing less than the saving truth proclaimed by the fourth evangelist: "But these are written that you may believe that Jesus is the Christ, the Son of God, and that believing you may have life in His name" (Jn 20:31).

To put it plainly, at this critical juncture in time, John the Baptist *does not believe* that Jesus is the Christ, the Son of God. Instead, he questions this truth. Does he then have eternal life? Of course.

It is precisely here that much evangelical thought suffers from thick theological cobwebs. We have already pointed out in an earlier chapter that the biblical portrait of saving faith is of an act of appropriation. This appropriation is the means by which both regeneration and justification become permanent realities for the believer.

Saving faith, we have seen, is like a single drink of living water which never needs to be repeated. It is like a single look at Jesus the Savior, much as the Israelites looked at the brazen serpent in the desert and lived. Saving faith is a decisive moment of spiritual hearing in which the voice of God's Son effects an irreversible spiritual resurrection.

We are not saved by drinking and drinking and drinking the water of life. We are saved simply by drinking it.

People are not saved by staring at Christ. They are saved by looking at Him in faith.

The songwriters have said it clearly:

> There is life in a look at the Crucified One,
> There is life at this moment for thee;
> Then look, sinner, look unto Him and be saved,
> Unto Him who was nailed to the tree.
>
> Look! look! look and live!
> There is life in a look at the Crucified One,
> There is life at this moment for thee.
> —Miss A. M. Hull and E. G. Taylor
> *There is Life in a Look*

John the Baptist was nearing the end of his earthly life. The "saving look" by which he had been born again was now well in the past. At the moment his perception of Jesus was clouded by uncertainty and confusion.

But he had not lost the gift of eternal life. "For the gifts and the calling of God are irrevocable" (Ro 11:29). Instead, John had only lost his shield. Fortunately, he had the good sense to ask our Lord to help him get it back again.

Did he get it back? Let us hope so. The words Jesus sent to him contained powerful reassurance (Lk 7:22). But let us also admit that the Scripture does not affirm that he did or did not recover his faith. The question is left open by Luke's narrative as well as by Matthew's parallel account (Mt 11:2–15). And where the Scriptures are silent, we must be silent too.

There are some, indeed, who hold the opinion that a lapse of faith such as John's can happen to a Christian but can only be temporary. Restoration to faith, we are assured, is inevitable for a truly born-again person.

We might be tempted to ask how long such a lapse in faith may continue: a day, a month, a year, two years? But there is no answer to a question like that. For that matter, the view that Christians can stop believing only for a while is a wholly unjustified theological dogma. It's biblical support is exactly zero.

Faith in Shipwreck

In the later years of his earthly life, Paul wrote two letters to Timothy, his younger associate in ministry. Among his many challenging words to this co-laborer, we find these:

> This charge I commit to you, son Timothy, according to the prophecies previously made concerning you, that by them you may *wage the good warfare*, holding faith and a good conscience, which some having rejected [or, pushed aside] *concerning the faith have suffered shipwreck*, of whom are Hymenaeus and Alexander, whom I have delivered to Satan that they may learn not to blaspheme (1Ti 1:18–20; italics added).

This Pauline text requires the very closest attention. "You are in a war, Timothy," Paul is telling him. "And if you want to wage a successful war you will need to hold on to faith and a good conscience. I know of some people who have pushed a good conscience aside and have thus suffered shipwreck in their Christian faith." (It should be pointed out that in the phrase "holding faith and a good conscience, which ... ," the word "which" in the original Greek has reference to the "good conscience.")

Paul, of course, was an experienced sea traveler and had already undergone literal shipwreck three times when he wrote his second letter to Corinth (2Co 11:25). An additional occasion is graphically described in Acts 27. Against such a seafaring background, when Paul wrote these words to Timothy, he probably had a specific nautical image in mind.

Though we cannot be certain of the exact form this image took for Paul, one suggestion in particular makes excellent sense. It may be that Paul thinks of "faith and a good conscience" as a pair of oars, both of which must be firmly held and rowed in unison if the boat is to be safely directed. But if one oar is pushed aside (the "good conscience" oar), the other oar (the "faith" oar) cannot be properly handled and the ship will head for dangerous reefs and shoals.

It need hardly be said that Paul would not have spoken this way to Timothy if he had felt that there was no danger for his younger friend. On the contrary, Paul knew perfectly well that Christians were not immune to the shipwreck of their faith.

Indeed, it is even quite clear that he regards Hymenaeus and Alexander as Christians who have gone astray. The language he uses of them makes this plain. Paul says that these two men have been "delivered to Satan." But this is precisely the language he employs of the immoral brother at Corinth who is to be excommunicated from church fellowship for his sin (1Co 5:1–5).

Equally pointed is his choice of the word "learn" to state the goal of their experience under Satan's harsh power. Actually, the Greek word in question is the one generally employed to describe the chastening or "child training" of Christians. It suggests both discipline and spiritual education. The word is so used by Paul himself (1Co 11:32), by the writer of Hebrews (12:6–11), and is found in Revelation on the lips of Jesus: "As many as I love, I rebuke and *chasten*" (Rev 3:19; italics added).

We may therefore render the idea Paul expresses like this: "I have turned these men over to Satan so that they may be educated not to blaspheme."

Once again we confront the down-to-earth realism of the Bible. The Christian's warfare is not a charade in which there are no defeats. The voyage of faith is not to be undertaken in the naive notion that shipwreck is impossible for a true believer.

We need the warnings of Scripture. And in a real sense we need to be told that there are some who fail—like Hymenaeus and Alexander.

Perhaps the Hymenaeus here is the same man Paul refers

to in his second letter to Timothy. Once again the apostle's words are illuminating:

> And their message will spread like cancer. Hymenaeus and Philetus are of this sort, who have strayed concerning the truth, saying that the resurrection is already past, *and they overthrow the faith of some.* Nevertheless the solid foundation of God stands, having this seal: *"The Lord knows those who are His,"* and, "Let everyone who names the name of Christ depart from iniquity" (2Ti 2:17–19; italics added).

If we are really talking about the same Hymenaeus in both passages, then the problem Paul mentions in 1 Timothy is clarified. Hymenaeus had gone astray doctrinally by claiming that the resurrection was not future, but past. Thus he had suffered shipwreck "concerning the faith." Moreover, Paul regarded his teaching about resurrection as a form of blasphemy which merited serious divine chastening. Hymenaeus was therefore turned over to the assaults of the enemy with the hope that he might be restored to a proper acknowledgment of the truth.

But even if the Hymenaeus mentioned in the second letter to Timothy is a different person, one fact emerges plainly from Paul's words. Hymenaeus's false doctrine about the resurrection had a destructive impact on the faith of some believers. He and Philetus, says Paul, "overthrow the faith of some."

To put it simply, Hymenaeus and Philetus either denied or reinterpreted the words Jesus spoke to Martha: "I am the resurrection. . . . He who believes in Me, though he may die, he shall live" (Jn 11:25). And they would have done the same to these words:

> This is the will of the Father who sent Me, that of all He has given Me I should lose nothing, but *should raise it up at the last day* (Jn 6:39; italics added; see v. 40).

Thus the doctrinal error of these two men struck at the very foundation of the Christian's hope. They denied the future resurrection which the Lord Jesus Christ Himself had promised to every believer.

And some Christians fell into their trap. Their faith in the promise of Jesus was overthrown.

Are we surprised by this? We shouldn't be. Nowhere does the Word of God guarantee that the believer's faith inevitably will endure.

What *does* it guarantee? That God's purposes are not defeated by the collapse of a Christian's convictions about the truth. It is precisely this fact that Paul now proceeds to affirm. "The foundation of God," insists the apostle, "stands firm." Moreover, like the base of an impressive monument, this foundation is inscribed with a twofold sealing inscription.

The first part of that inscription is a declaration that the believer's basic relationship to God is unaffected by the overthrow of one's faith. Paul writes, "The Lord knows those who are His."

What a reassuring word this is! If, indeed, on the spiritual battlefield believers should lose their shield, they may no longer know in their own heart that they belong to Christ. But even if they do not know, the Lord does! That is what really counts.[3]

But the second half of the inscription is equally potent. Let it be noted that the statement Paul now makes is not a prediction but rather a command. "Let everyone who names the name of Christ depart from iniquity."

Undoubtedly, the Christian who has lost his or her faith may cease to name the name of Christ, and may even cease to confess Christianity. But that is not an invitation to slackness on the part of those who still name that name.

On the contrary, God's demand is the same for them no matter whose faith is overthrown. They should depart from iniquity. Of course, this command is as broad as the word "iniquity" itself. Nevertheless, as the context shows, Paul has especially in mind the iniquity of doctrine that subverts the truth (2Ti 2:14–16, 20–26).

Let there be no mistake. The failure of one's faith is a grim possibility on the field of spiritual battle. To deny this is to be spiritually unprepared for the enemy's assault.

But equally, to acknowledge it is not in any way an invitation to fall prey to satanic falsehoods—far from it. The

Commander still challenges us to stand firm against our foe. He still commands allegiance to His truth.

His call still rings in our ears: "Let everyone who names the name of Christ depart from iniquity."

Conclusion

It has been said that Hudson Taylor, the great man of faith who founded the China Inland Mission, held 2 Timothy 2:13 to be one of the pivotal verses of his life. The words of that verse come shortly before the passage we have just considered. Paul's statement there is memorable. He writes: "If we are faithless [KJV = "believe not"], He remains faithful; He cannot deny Himself" (2Ti 2:13).

From this profound assertion Hudson Taylor drew tremendous strength. Through it he came to realize that the faithfulness of God was independent of his own personal trust in that faithfulness. Even when Taylor did *not* believe, God was still faithful!

Too many Christians tend to feel that the reality of their experience with God depends on the firmness of their faith. It is true, of course, that we are saved through an act of faith. Thereby we appropriate a gift that is absolutely free. But once this transaction occurs, the reality of our salvation is quite independent of our confidence in that reality.

In other words, the Lord Jesus Christ has made firm promises to us. When we trust Him, He guarantees that we possess eternal life (Jn 6:47)—that we will not come into judgment (Jn 5:24)—that He will raise us up at the last day (Jn 6:39–40). And even if we stop believing all this, *He remains faithful!*[4]

For Him to renege on such promises would be nothing less than a denial of His own character and fidelity. But, as the apostle points out, *He cannot deny Himself.*

Does this truth weaken our hands in the battle? Of course not. In fact, as Hudson Taylor learned, it actually strengthens our heart for the conflict which lies before us.

It will help us greatly to realize that God's truth is true even when we fail to believe it. Reality is not focused within ourselves as though our faith could create or destroy that reality. Instead, reality remains constant. Faith is simply acceptance of God's testimony about reality. But if we reject that testimony, reality itself is completely unaffected.

We need to keep this perspective in view. Knowing this helps us to hold the shield of faith more firmly.

10

THE CHOICE IS YOURS

10

The Choice Is Yours

In a vivid passage, one which we have already reviewed briefly, the apostle Peter exhorts his Christian readers to develop their faith. So important is this process, that he urges them to apply "all diligence" to get it done.

According to Peter, when God saved us, "His divine power" gave us everything we need for "life and godliness" (2Pe 1:3). God expects us, therefore, to draw on these resources to produce a productive Christian experience.

Thus we are to be diligent to add virtue to our Christian faith (2Pe 1:5), but we are not to stop there. Knowledge, Peter tells us, as well as self-control, perseverance, godliness, brotherly kindness, and love must also be added (1:5–7). Each quality, in fact, is added to the other like a series of building blocks being stacked one upon another.

In speaking this way, of course, the apostle clearly has in mind the mature, fully developed Christian character which God expects each believer to build onto the foundation of their faith. In fact, after saying this, Peter writes these significant words: "For if these things are yours and abound, they keep you from being either barren or unfruitful in the knowledge of our Lord Jesus Christ" (2Pe 1:8).

"The key to Christian fruitfulness," asserts the apostle, "is found in the very qualities I have just told you to add to your faith. With these things present and abounding in your experience, you will by no means live a barren or unproductive life."

117

Yet once again, like all the other New Testament writers, Peter takes nothing for granted in the Christian's pursuit of holiness. To be sure, it is highly desirable that no believer should be "barren or unfruitful." The qualities the apostle has named, if added to the life, will guarantee that he or she is not.

But Peter can conceive of an alternative situation as well. He describes it this way: "For he who lacks these things is blind, cannot see afar off, and has forgotten that he was purged [= cleansed] from his old sins" (2Pe 1:9).

It goes without saying that the apostle is not speaking here of unsaved people. *Of course* unsaved people do not possess these spiritual qualities. Peter does not need to state that. Instead, he is clearly thinking of a saved person, for the kind of individual he has in mind has experienced God's forgiveness, and has been "cleansed from his old sins."

But, regrettably, such a person has lost any awareness of God's forgiving grace in days gone by. Where once there was spiritual vision, now there is shortsightedness and loss of perception. And this is precisely because the precious qualities that make a believer fruitful are tragically lacking.

Obviously, where these qualities are missing, so also is the fruit.

How strange that in our day and time we have been told so often that fruitlessness is a sure sign that a person is unsaved. Certainly we did not get this idea from the Bible. Rather, the Bible teaches that unfruitfulness in a believer is a sure sign that one is no longer moving forward, no longer growing in Christ. It is a sign that the Christian is spiritually sick, and until well again, cannot enjoy spiritual success.

By contrast, lordship thought subtly baptizes the American success ethic into the church. God, we are told in effect, is the God only of the spiritually successful. Only a triumphant believer can really be sure of God's love.

But what about the tragic history of the nation of Israel? Was God not really involved with them? Is His name hopelessly disgraced because they failed? Of course not.

Indeed, the same theology that tells us that God tolerates only limited failures inside His family often also tells us something else. It often tells us that Christ would not really die for the sins of people who will ultimately reject Him. Thus, on this view, our Lord died only for the elect and not for the whole world.

The problem here is simple. Lordship thought does not understand the real nature of grace. It does not understand that God is capable of generously loving men and women who are ultimate disappointments to Him. Lordship theology is comfortable only with the legal prescription, "This do and thou shalt live."

No one can be happy that there are Christians who fit the description Peter gives us in 1:9 of his second letter. But nothing is gained by denying this reality, and much can be lost by doing so.

If our warfare cannot be fought effectively without facing the possibility of defeat, the same is true here as well. Fruitfulness is not automatic in the Christian life. Rather, it is the product of applying "all diligence" (1:5) to the development of a well-rounded, productive Christian character.

There are no shortcuts. There are no easy formulas. And if we fail to be diligent, as Peter commands us to be, we can soon find ourselves roaming a spiritual wasteland where the rich fruits of Christian experience are not to be found. But if we face this danger frankly, we can avoid it.

The Danger of Inactivity

One of the warning signs that Scripture has clearly posted for us is the danger of spiritual inactivity. Those who ignore this warning can soon find their lives blasted by the chill winds of unproductivity and fruitlessness.

We have already noticed Paul's words to Titus urging him to exhort believers to "be careful to maintain good works" (Tit 3:8). But this is not an isolated theme with Paul, and in a truly memorable passage he also writes this:

> Therefore, my beloved brethren, be steadfast, immovable, *always abounding in the work of the Lord,* inasmuch as you know that your labor is not in vain in the Lord (1Co 15:58; italics added).

We should note the context for these words. They follow a long discussion in which Paul reaffirms the truth of a future, physical resurrection (15:1–57). If that truth is lost by his readers, then their motivation for maintaining good works will be subverted (15:32). Indeed, their very faith in Christ may be overturned like those who, later, gave ear to Hymenaeus and Philetus (2Ti 2:17–19). Paul's exhortation is born of genuine concern.

And like the apostle Peter, Paul too was well aware that Christians could lapse into unfruitfulness. Consequently, addressing Titus again, he said this: "And let our people also learn to maintain good works, to meet urgent needs, *that they may not be unfruitful*" (Tit 3:14; italics added).

The wasteland of barren living was therefore a real and present danger which the New Testament writers faced with candor. In no way did they share the modern illusion that a believer could not enter that wasteland, or live there. Since Christian living was an intense spiritual warfare, the inspired writers knew perfectly well that there could be casualties. That was one thing which made them the effective pastors that they were.

But of all of the New Testament authors, the one who most emphatically warned against spiritual inertia was James, the half brother of our Lord. His teaching on this theme was vivid and unforgettable.

Naturally, James knew that he and his readers were born again. In fact, he says so: "Of His own will He brought us forth by the word of truth" (Jas 1:18). But he also knew how urgently he and they needed always to be ready to respond to God's Word.

For that reason, James wrote as follows: "Therefore lay aside all filthiness and overflow of wickedness, and receive with meekness the implanted word, which is able to save your souls" (Jas 1:21).

We must be careful not to misunderstand these words. In modern English, the phrase "to save your souls" has for many people only one religious meaning. It means "to be saved from hell."

But this is *not* what it meant to James or to any of his readers. In the Greek language in which James was writing, this was a standard phrase meaning "to save your lives." Never in the entire Bible—in the Old Testament or New— did this phrase mean "to save from hell." And it does not mean that here.

James is talking to born-again believers (1:18), in whom the living seed of God's Word has been "implanted" by regeneration. He has been warning them, moreover, about the fact that sin, if pursued to its end, can culminate in physical death (1:15). He would have agreed heartily with Paul that "if you live according to the flesh you will die" (Ro 8:13a).

But it did not need to be so. If his readers would lay aside any besetting wickedness, and if they would meekly receive God's Word, their lives could be spared from a premature and untimely death through sin. In the spirit of the book of Proverbs, James believed that "the fear of the Lord prolongs days, but the years of the wicked will be shortened" (Prov 10:27; see 11:19; 12:28; 13:14; 19:16).

Once again, James would have approved of Paul's declaration, "but if you through the Spirit put to death the deeds of the body, you will live" (Ro 8:13b).[1]

But to enjoy the "life-saving" benefits of God's implanted Word, there was one simple, but completely indispensable, condition. James states it plainly in the following verse: "But be doers of the word, and not hearers only, deceiving yourselves" (1:22).

It is not enough, says James, for the Christian simply to receive God's Word. It is not enough merely to hear its instruction. To benefit from it—to prolong one's life by means of it—one must also *do* it.

In other words, activity is required. Obedience is utterly essential if one wishes to reap the blessings God's truth can bring to us.

So James continues:

> For if anyone is a hearer of the word and not a doer, he is like a man observing his natural face in a mirror; for he observes himself, goes away, and immediately forgets what kind of man he was (1:23–24).

Every Christian knows what James is talking about. How easy it is to listen to an inspiring biblical message, to see in the mirror of God's truth what I really am and ought to be as a believer in Jesus Christ, and yet to walk out of church and forget all about it. And by Monday morning it is just as if I had never heard that message at all.

"Don't be like that," James is saying. "Act on God's truth and thus enjoy its blessings."

> But he who looks into the perfect law of liberty and continues in it, and is not a forgetful hearer but *a doer of the work,* this one will be blessed in what he does (1:25; italics added).

There is no other way. Eternal life is God's good and perfect gift to us (Jas 1:17–18). It is absolutely free. But God's blessing on our Christian experience requires *work.* To make progress in the faith, the believer must do more than just listen to God's truth.

The believer needs to obey it.

The Danger of Dead Orthodoxy

But what if the believer does not? What are the consequences of repeated failure to act on God's gracious, life-preserving Word? Here, too, James has something to say to us.

Like all the New Testament authors, James shared with his readers a high view of faith. He was perfectly aware that people are justified by faith apart from works, and he is completely at home with the great Pauline proof text about Abraham's justification (Ge 15:6; Jas 2:23).

But James also understood how easily Christians, who knew the great truth that God accepted us on the basis of faith alone, could fall into the error of downplaying good works altogether. He understood how readily doctrinal correctness could take precedence over practical, everyday obedience. In short, he knew the danger of dead orthodoxy.

Naturally, on the field of spiritual battle, our satanic enemy is eager to strike the shield of faith out of our hands. We have already discussed this fact in the previous chapter. A Christian deprived of that shield is at high risk in the conflict with the Devil. He or she has no means of quenching the opponent's fiery darts.

But Satan has more than one method of assault. If the shield cannot be dislodged from our grip, its effectiveness may still be neutralized in other ways. And one way this may be done is to get us to lock it up in our theological armory so that we never employ it on the battlefield of everyday living.

Sadly, all too many times in the history of the church, Christians have turned their faith into a stiff and brittle creed which had little relevance to their daily experiences. While proudly proclaiming their own orthodoxy, and ungraciously denouncing those who believed differently, they talked like theologians and behaved like brutes.

Something like that was going on in the church or churches to which James was writing. James speaks searingly of the "wars and fights" that occurred among his readers (4:1). And although as Christians they could have come to God to meet their needs, they did not do so. Or if they did, their requests were denied because those requests were selfish: "You fight and war. Yet you do not have because you do not ask. You ask and do not receive, because you ask amiss, that you may spend it on your pleasures" (Jas 4:2–3).

It is not a pretty picture. Yet it is a picture of *Christians*, whose privilege of prayer James here clearly takes for granted.[a] If they would only ask correctly, they would receive.

Naturally, as might be expected, the tongue was a major weapon in these intramural wars. James spends nearly a whole chapter warning about the damage this tiny physical instrument can cause (3:1–12). Do his readers wish to prove themselves wise? Let them not use their tongues to do so. There is a better way: "Who is wise and understanding among you? Let him show *by good conduct that his works are done in the meekness of wisdom*" (3:13; italics added).

"Words do not really prove you wise," James is saying, "but good works do." What advice could be better? It's essence was simple: "Talk less, and obey more!"

But how devastatingly barren was the opposite condition. James describes it pointedly:

But if you have bitter envy and self-seeking in your hearts, do not boast and lie against the truth. This wisdom does not descend from above, but is earthly, sensual, demonic. For where envy and self-seeking exist, confusion and every evil thing will be there (3:14–16).

Let there be no mistaking James's point. Inside the Christian family, the presence of envy and self-seeking results not merely in barrenness, but in "confusion and every evil thing." Only if his brethren were controlled by "the wisdom that is from above" would their experience be "full of mercy and good fruits" (3:17).

And he adds: "The fruit of righteousness is sown in peace by those who make peace" (3:18).

Can anyone be surprised that to Christian readers such as these James offers scathing condemnation for a faith which is inoperative and unproductive?

No doubt in their discussions with one another, these believers often made impressive claims to faith. But how effective was that faith in daily life? Could their faith, all by itself, save their lives from the death-dealing consequences of sin which James has pointedly described earlier in his letter (1:13–15)?

Of course not. James puts it bluntly: "What does it profit, *my brethren,* if someone says he has faith but does not have works? That faith cannot save him, can it?" (2:14; italics added).

The question, "Can faith save him?" is expressed by James in Greek in a form that anticipates a negative response. It can be rendered, "Faith can't save him, can it?" The expected reply is: "No, indeed!"

It is precisely here that many readers and expositors of James have gone tragically astray. To begin with, they often miss the obvious point that James clearly means to say that faith *cannot save* the man he is describing.

But James is not talking here about salvation from hell. *Why should he?* He and his readers were born again (1:18), they had faith in the Lord of glory (2:1), they had the privileges of prayer (4:2–3), and he repeatedly calls them his brethren (1:2, 9, 16, 19; 2:1, 5, 14–15; 3:1, 10, 12; 4:11; 5:7, 9–10, 12, 19).

James had no need whatsoever to discuss with his brethren the issue of salvation from hell. Those who think otherwise do not understand the perfect freeness of the gift of life as James understood it (1:17–18).[3]

But, as we have seen, James did need to discuss the truth that God's Word could save his Christian readers from the death-dealing consequences of sin (1:15, 21). And he has already insisted that *this kind* of salvation can only be effected by obedience—by good works (1:22–25). Thus it is to this truth—and to this truth alone—that James is referring when he inquires, "Faith can't save him, now can it?"

No, it cannot. If we speak of prolonging human life by godliness, we are speaking of something faith alone cannot achieve. If we speak, as the writer of Proverbs did, of escaping "the snares of death," we are talking about the result of obedient conduct (Prov 13:14).

But faith which is no longer expressed in practical and obedient ways is an ineffectual faith on the battleground of life. Indeed, such faith may itself be described as "dead" (2:17, 20, 26). It is the same as saying that a creed on which we have ceased to act is nothing more than dead orthodoxy.

Conclusion

In the closing verse of his famous discussion about faith and works, James writes: "For as the body without the spirit is dead, so faith without works is dead also" (Jas 2:26).

If I were walking down the street one day and encountered a dead body, I could easily conclude two things. First, I could conclude that the body no longer contained its life-giving spirit, and second, that this body had once actually been alive. One thing I would most certainly not conclude. I would not conclude that the body had never been alive at all.

Yet, in one of the strangest distortions of Scripture that has ever occurred, many theologians and Bible interpreters have decided that a "dead faith" must necessarily have always been dead.

But why draw such a deduction as this? James compares

"dead faith" to a dead body. Surely this was not a loose or careless analogy on his part. If "dead faith" had never been alive, why not compare it to a stone or some other inanimate object?

But clearly, James has chosen this analogy precisely because it is especially suited to make his point. What James is worried about is a Christian whose faith has lost all of its vitality and productiveness. He is worried about the man or woman whose faith has ceased to move and act, just as a dead body has ceased to move and act.

Like the apostle Peter, James can conceive of a Christian who lacks the spiritual qualities that need to be added to one's faith (2Pe 1:5–9). And also like Peter, he censures this condition as tragic and appalling.

For Peter, such a person was "shortsighted, even to blindness" and had "forgotten that he was purged from his old sins." For James, such a person—for all the loud claims to correct belief—has a faith that is no more vital than a physical corpse.

Strong words, to be sure. But necessary words. Only by calling spiritual abnormalities by their true names—only by confronting spiritual sickness for what it really is—only thus can such conditions be corrected.

In fact, only thus can they be avoided in the first place. For what I deem impossible for myself, I thereby make more difficult to elude. A danger unseen is a danger increased.

So, at least, Peter thought when he wrote these words:

> You therefore, beloved, *seeing you know these things beforehand,* beware lest you also, being led away with the error of the wicked, fall from your own steadfastness (2Pe 3:17; italics added).

"Be warned!" says the apostle. "Be aware of the danger. Otherwise you might fall from your own steadfastness. Otherwise you might be led astray into wicked paths."

But once again, it did not need to be so. Consider the beautiful alternative: "But grow in the grace and knowledge of our Lord and Savior Jesus Christ" (2Pe 3:18).

"The choice," says the apostle, "is yours."

11

DINING WITH JESUS

11

Dining With Jesus

In words that have struck a responsive chord down through the years of Christian history, Jesus invited Himself to dinner. His winsome declaration is recorded in the last of the letters to the seven churches of Asia: "Behold, I stand at the door and knock. If anyone hears My voice and opens the door, I will come in to him and dine with him, and He with Me" (Rev 3:20).

It would be wrong to take this famous statement as a simple gospel invitation, though that has often been done. Here our Lord is addressing a Christian church and, clearly, anyone in the church is invited to respond.

Of course this was the church of Laodicea, famous for its character as a lukewarm congregation. That state of affairs, however, should not surprise us. We have already seen repeatedly how the New Testament writers faced squarely the reality of believers living below the standards God had set for them. And by facing this reality, they sought to alter or prevent it.

Accordingly, we can detect precisely this outlook in our Lord's words to the Laodicean church. Here was a group of believers who boasted in their material wealth, but were spiritually impoverished (Rev 3:17–18). Though they had works (3:15a), in character they were like tepid water. They neither stimulated through warmth nor braced and refreshed through an invigorating coolness (3:15b).

The result was that their very existence as a church body

was in jeopardy. Designed as were all the churches for service as the mouth of God—that is, to be an instrument for proclaiming His truth—this role could be forfeited. Like some unpalatable draught of liquid, they could find themselves spewed forth from the lips of their Lord (3:16). They could lose their privilege as His mouthpiece to the world.

But another possibility lay ready at hand. The Lord says to them: "As many as I love, I rebuke and chasten [or, child-train]. Therefore be zealous and repent" (Rev 3:19).

The Laodiceans were wayward children of God. But the love of their Savior pursued them and "child-trained" them in the way that His faithfulness required. Solemnly, He called them to repent of their lukewarm spirit and to renew their intimacy with Him.

He stood, therefore, on the threshold of their lives. With His rebukes He spoke to them, and with His discipline He knocked on the door of their hearts. But it was up to them to respond. It was for them to open the door to Him. And if they did, He would dine with them and they would dine with Him. But the choice was theirs. He would not break down their door.

As simple as this observation sounds, however, it cannot be stressed too much. Of course, in His sovereignty, God could impose Himself on every Christian person. Indeed, He could do so with every individual in the world. He could compel everyone everywhere to love Him.

But of what value would that be to God? What worth is there in a love that is coerced? Is it not the very essence of love that, if it is to be real, it must be given freely? What parent worthy of the name does not desire their children's love? But, by the same token, what sensible parent wishes to compel that love, even if that were possible? Indeed, in every relationship in life—whether parent and child, husband and wife, or friend and friend—the value of all love rests in its spontaneity and freeness.

This, too, lordship theology does not understand. In the mistaken notion that they are serving the divine interest, lordship teachers affirm that no true Christian fails to love God. If they are asked how this could be true when man is notoriously fickle and shifting in his affections, the answer always boils down to one thing: God guarantees it.

If that is so then that love is no longer spontaneous. It is no longer free. Indeed, it is actually no longer real love. Like the Christian race itself, like the warfare of the Christian life, our love for God—in lordship thought—becomes a mere charade, a mere shadow of the spontaneous reality it is supposed to represent.

The Bible does not teach this sort of thing. The scriptural revelation knows nothing of a doctrine in which Christian love for God is guaranteed by the mere fact that one is a Christian.

To be sure, the *capacity* to love both God and people is imparted to us at new birth. It is obviously included in the "all things that pertain to life and godliness" which were bestowed upon us when we trusted Christ (2Pe 1:3). But it is also true that "brotherly kindness" and "love" stand at the very pinnacle of the Christian character we are urged to build with "all diligence" (2Pe 1:5). To put it plainly, the capacity to love must be nurtured and developed.

With God's help, it can be.

Fellowship With Christ

The words Jesus spoke to the Laodicean Christians were clearly a call to personal fellowship with Himself. In the ancient Middle East, sharing one's table with others was a fundamental and basic way of having communion with them. It was the very essence of hospitality and a signal of personal acceptance. On the other hand, to intrude on a dinner situation uninvited was an insensitive affront to the host.

But the concept of dining with the Savior is only one reflection of a rich biblical truth which we meet elsewhere. Indeed, our Lord's words to Laodicea have their roots in the teaching He gave to His disciples in the Upper Room. For, in those precious, final hours of table fellowship with their Teacher before He died, the eleven disciples were told this:

> He who has My commandments and keeps them, it is he who loves Me. And he who loves Me will be loved by My Father, and I will love him and manifest Myself to him (Jn 14:21).

Let it be noted that the audience for these words included only regenerate men. Judas Iscariot had already departed (13:26–30). The call to obedience, therefore, is issued to the Lord's born-again disciples. And this call is accompanied by a promise. The obedient disciple will experience the love of both the Father and the Son and, beyond that, will experience a self-disclosure from the Son: "I will... manifest Myself to him."

The disciples do not understand these words, however. Their whole concept of the disclosure of the Messiah was rooted in their anticipation of His public manifestation in power and glory. Perplexed, one of them asks for clarification: "Judas (not Iscariot) said to Him, 'Lord, how is it that You will manifest Yourself to us, and not to the world?'" (Jn 14:22.)

What sort of experience might this be? the disciples are wondering. Is the Messiah's glory to be made visible to them in some kind of spectacular, private display?

Their Teacher's answer is illuminating. This was not to be a collective experience even for this inner circle of men. Instead, it was an intensely personal and individual experience to which each of them must make the appropriate response:

> Jesus answered and said to him, "If *anyone* loves Me, *he* will keep My word; and My Father will love *him*, and We will come to *him* and make Our home with *him*" (Jn 14:23; italics added).

Thus, like the words to Laodicea, the call to communion is individualized. To Laodicea Jesus says, "If *anyone* hears ... and opens" (Rev 3:20). And to the Eleven, He says, "If *anyone* loves Me, *he*. . . ." And in both passages He says—in effect—"I will come in to *him*."

The Lord Jesus Christ, therefore, offers Himself to individual believers as a divine Guest. If they will respond to Him, if they will love and obey Him, He will make their hearts and lives His personal habitation so that their experience will be like having supper with their Savior. Across the common "table" which they share, they can communicate freely and He can make Himself known to them. He can *manifest* Himself to them.

This concept is not to be confused with the glorious truth that Christ indwells every believer by His Spirit (Ro 8:9–10). By no means can our relationships to an infinite Lord be reduced to one simple formulation, however impressive. Rather, these relationships are many-faceted and complex. Yes, our bodies *are* the temple of God (1Co 6:19–20). But our *lives*—our earthly experiences—can likewise become His place of residence: "We will make Our *home* with him"!

The apostle Paul of course knew this truth as well, and he expressed it in his own memorable way:

> For this reason I bow my knees to the Father of our Lord Jesus Christ . . . that He would grant you . . . to be strengthened with might by His Spirit in the inner man, *that Christ may dwell in your hearts by faith* . . . (Eph 3:14, 16–17).

But did not Christ already dwell in their hearts? Most assuredly He did. Yet Paul can conceive of a special kind of inner experience of the Savior, which he associated with inward, spiritual strength (Eph 3:16) and with "being rooted and grounded in love" (Eph 3:17b).

So he prayed for that experience for his fellow believers. That special experience was not automatically theirs simply because they were Christians. Paul never dreamed that this lovely spiritual experience was an inevitable consequence of their conversion.

Nor did our Lord Himself take anything for granted in addressing the eleven disciples. "*If* anyone loves Me, . . ." said the Savior. But there was an obvious, and sobering, alternative: "He who does not love Me does not keep My words; and the word which you hear is not Mine but the Father's who sent Me" (Jn 14:24).

"The test of a person's love for me," says Jesus, "is obedience to my words. And please remember that if you disobey my words, you are actually disobeying the words of my Father."

Surely this is as clear as possible. The exchange Jesus has is with regenerate men, but they still need to be told that their love for Him is measured—not by their verbal claims to it—but by their actual obedience to His Word.

Peter, in particular, had made great protestations of love that night (Jn 13:37). But before the evening had ended, not only Peter, but all the disciples, "forsook Him and fled" (Mt 26:56).

No, love is not an automatic response which every believer inevitably gives to God. The Christian is not a robot who has been programmed to love the Lord and who can do nothing but what he or she was programmed to do. The very thought is unnatural and abhorrent.

God did not create machines. He created real flesh-and-blood human beings. And when humankind fell in the Garden of Eden and lost the capacity to love their Maker, God redeemed them through the cross and re-imparted this capacity to every believer in Christ. Now He calls His children to the kind of loving obedience which is rooted in a gift of life that is absolutely free. "We love Him because He first loved us" (1Jn 4:19).

But God Himself loves *us* freely and He loves *us* with infinite spontaneity. So He obviously desires that our love for Him should mirror His own for us and be spontaneous in return.

For that reason, in the New Testament Scriptures, God seeks our love. He encourages and invites it, and He promises to meet it with an experience of rich fellowship with Himself.

He desires our love greatly, to be sure. But He will never compel it: "Behold, I stand at the door and knock."

The Abiding Life

Not long after our Lord spoke to His disciples the words on which we have been reflecting, He and they left the Upper Room. "Arise, let us go from here," He said (Jn 14:31), and thus that final supper, with all its rich spiritual fellowship, came to an end.

No doubt Jesus and the disciples had arrived at the Mount of Olives, dotted as it was with vineyards and orchards, when the next recorded words were spoken:

I am the true vine, and My Father is the vinedresser. Every branch in Me that does not bear fruit He takes away; and every branch that bears fruit He prunes, that it may bear more fruit. . . Abide in Me, and I in you. As the branch cannot bear fruit of itself, unless it abides in the vine, neither can *you*, unless *you* abide in Me (Jn 15:1–2, 4).

Few passages in the New Testament are more resolutely opposed to lordship doctrine than this one. Only by a grotesque distortion of its obvious intent and meaning can it be made, even awkwardly, to fit into the lordship pattern of thought.

Once again, eleven regenerate men are its only audience. But so far is our Lord from assuming that these men will inevitably bear fruit, that He actually urges them to "abide" in Him for that very purpose. Of course, as we know too well, before the night went much further, all had ceased to do so! As Matthew writes (26:56), "Then all the disciples forsook Him and fled."

It is striking that when Jesus said earlier, "We will . . . make Our home with him" (14:23), He used a Greek word related to the word "abide." In effect He had said, "We will . . . make our 'abiding place' with him"!

So the truths involved here are inseparably intertwined. They are indeed one truth.

In the Upper Room the Lord had taught these men that obedience to His commands would bring with it the experience of His Father and Himself "abiding" in their lives. Now, on the slopes of Olivet, He changes the visual image as He communicates precisely the same truth.

The relationship that these men had to Him as His disciples could be compared, Jesus said, to a vine/branch relationship. And just as in the horticulture of vineyards, where branches could be severed from their vines, so too this could transpire in the experience of His disciples as well. If that happened, fruitfulness would cease. Hence, the disciples must be careful to "abide" in the True Vine.

As is well known, however, many have read the metaphor of the vine and the branches as though it described the state of salvation. They have then concluded that salvation can be lost, since a branch can obviously be separated from the vine.

But this is utterly without warrant in the gospel of John. It is even incredible that anyone could read the first twelve chapters of this book with any attentiveness at all and then come to such a conclusion. We have already seen how often, and how emphatically, the fourth evangelist teaches that the gift of eternal life can never be lost, and we need not repeat that discussion here.

Suffice it to say, the view that John 15 teaches the possible loss of salvation flies directly into the face of John's theology. It cannot possibly be right.

But the lordship position on this text is even more confused. Lordship teachers also usually view the abiding relationship as a description of the state of salvation.[1] But the command to abide implies that the alternative—not abiding—is possible. Yet, in most lordship teaching, "not abiding" is not really possible for a truly regenerate person. Thus, the command to Christians to abide once again reduces itself to a charade. Every Christian does it anyway.

Even worse, John 15:6 speaks about a branch which has been severed from the vine, becomes withered, and is actually burned. But what can this possibly mean within the premises of lordship thought? If the vine/branch relationship describes the state of salvation, then no unsaved person was ever a branch to begin with. How, then, can such a person be described as a branch that is withered and burned? Clearly, in John 15, lordship theology leads its proponents into a hopeless quagmire.

It is a serious—and totally unnecessary—mistake to view the vine/branch metaphor as a picture of salvation. Nothing at all in the text suggests this.

On the contrary, the text does suggest that the metaphor is related to discipleship. Thus, in His final words about this significant analogy, Jesus says: "By this My Father is glorified, that you bear much fruit; *so you will be My disciples*" (Jn 15:8; italics added).

We have already observed that discipleship is basically the experience of *spiritual education*. It is a process which can and should begin immediately after we are born again, by faith, into the family of God. But we have also seen that, unlike our permanent membership in God's family, discipleship is an experience in which we are responsible to persist. With God's help, we are to see it through to the end.

Born-again people, therefore—people like the eleven to whom Jesus was speaking—need to learn that the secret of discipleship is to cultivate an "abiding" relationship with their Teacher. If they do this, our Lord affirms, they will bring glory to God by their fruitfulness. And in so doing, they will indeed be His "pupils" since He too glorified the Father in this way.

But what if the Christian disciple does not abide in Christ? The result is expressed in verse 6: "If anyone does not abide in Me, he is cast out as a branch and is withered; and they gather them, and throw them into the fire, and they are burned" (Jn 15:6).

This statement has caused needless perplexity. The main reason for that is the strong impulse many readers have to identify the reference to fire with hell. But this is an unjustified interpretive leap. There is no reason at all to think of the fire as literal, just as we are not dealing with a literal vine, literal branches, or literal fruit. "Fire" here is simply another figurative element in the horticultural metaphor.

What happened, therefore, in vineyards all over Palestine, could happen to the disciples as well. If they failed to "abide" in Jesus, they would be separated from their experience of fellowship with Him: they would be "cast out as [or, like] a branch." Intimate contact with the True Vine would be lost. But more, this loss of vital communion with the True Vine would result in the "drying up" of their spiritual experience: they would be "withered." And finally, they would be cast into the "fire" of trial and divine chastisement: "they gather them and throw them into the fire, and they are burned."

There is nothing unique about this kind of description. It is simply a vivid portrayal of a spiritual state which the New Testament describes in various ways.

For Peter, this can be the Christian who "lacks" the crucial qualities of Christian character and who "is blind, cannot see afar off, and has forgotten that he was purged from his old sins" (2Pe 1:9). For James, it can be the Christian who lacks works and whose faith is no longer vital and alive (Jas 2:14–26). And for Paul, it can be the Christian who has rejected "a good conscience" and has "suffered shipwreck" in regard to the faith (1Ti 1:19). Such a Christian may be "delivered to Satan" that he or she may "learn" the spiritual lessons they need to learn (1Ti 1:20).

Like all illustrations, of course, even the vine/branch metaphor has its limits. It can certainly portray divine chastening as a fire, just as the Old Testament frequently described God's temporal judgments on His people Israel under the same image (Pss 79:5; 89:46; Isa 10:17–19; Jer 4:4; 7:20; 15:14; 17:27; etc.).[2] But what the metaphor cannot do is to speak of restoration.

In a literal vineyard a severed branch cannot be restored to its place in the vine. Still less can it do so after being burned. But in the experience of Christian disciples, restoration to fellowship with Christ remains open to those who seek it. Indeed, "if we confess our sins, He is faithful and just to forgive us our sins and to cleanse us from all unrighteousness" (1Jn 1:9).

True, all eleven disciples broke contact with the True Vine that very night. But all eleven were also restored. And their future lives were rich with good fruit.

Conclusion

It was on this very night, to which the gospel writers devote so much space, that Jesus spoke words of solemn warning to a self-confident Peter.

> And the Lord said, "Simon, Simon! Indeed, Satan has asked to have you, that he may sift you as wheat. But I have prayed for you, that your faith should not fail, and when you have TURNED AGAIN, strengthen your brethren" (Lk 22:31–32; emphasis added).

Tragically, this warning went unheeded. Peter's reply brushes aside any prospect of failure on his part: "And he said to Him, 'Lord, I am ready to go with You, both to prison and to death'" (Lk 22:33).

"Count on me!" says Peter. "I love you enough to share prison with You, or even to die for You!"

Not long afterward, Jesus and the Eleven left the table fellowship of the Upper Room and came to the Mount of Olives. There, as we have seen, the Lord gave His disciples yet another word of warning.

"Abide in Me," He told them. But the Greek word for "abide" basically means to "stay" somewhere. So the Savior was saying, "Stay in Me. Don't let your link with Me be broken!"

Again, shortly afterward, they came to Gethsemane and our Lord issued still another warning: "Pray that you may not enter into temptation [or, testing]" (Lk 22:46).

And when He returned from His agonizing experience of prayer, He warns them for the final time: "Why do you sleep? Rise and pray, lest you enter into temptation [or, testing]" (Lk 22:46).

What followed is familiar to all readers of the Bible. What is less well known is that these events fulfill precisely John 15:6 in the lives of the Eleven. And for this, Peter is the classic case in point.

Contact with the True Vine is broken as Peter and the rest desert their Teacher. How different that night might have been for them if they had marched boldly at His side! But the branches were now severed from that True Vine and in their withered and weakened condition this is soon manifest in the events that take place next.

With skill the "fire" of testing and temptation has been ignited by the Devil. As our Lord had foreseen, Satan sifts Peter with his winnowing instrument just as a thresher of grain might sift wheat. So severe, in fact, is the satanic assault that Peter's faith might not have survived the attack— it might have been consumed in the fire! But his Master's intercessory prayer was heard and his faith did not fail (Lk 22:32).

But Peter himself failed. In the process he denied His Lord three times. Yet by the grace of God, Peter was also restored. His tears of regret (Lk 22:62) were indeed the first step in his "return" to Christ (Lk 22:32) and to a renewed experience of abiding in the True Vine.

Peter in fact repented. That's what the Laodiceans needed to do, too. Jesus Himself told them so: "As many as I love, I rebuke and chasten. Therefore be zealous and repent" (Rev 3:19). And if they did, they would be opening the door to intimate fellowship with Himself. He and they would dine together. Jesus wanted that experience with the Laodicean Christians just as surely as He wanted it with the eleven disciples. And He wants it with us as well.

But at every step of the way we must make the choices without which this privilege cannot be realized or maintained. If we are walking with Him, we must choose to stay with Him. If we lose touch with Him, we must choose to repent and turn to Him.

But until we do, He waits for us: "Behold, I stand at the door and knock."

12

REPENTANCE

12

Repentance

Peter repented. We can only hope that so did the Laodice-ans. In fact, the call to repent is also issued to the church at Ephesus (Rev 2:5), to the church at Pergamos (2:16), and to the church at Sardis (3:3).

On another occasion, the Christians at Corinth repented. Paul describes their repentance like this:

> For though I made you sorry with my letter, I do not regret it; though I did regret it. For I perceive that the same epistle has made you sorry, though only for a while. Now I rejoice, not that you were made sorry, but that your sorrow *led to repentance*. For you were made sorry in a godly manner, that you might suffer loss from us in nothing (2Co 7.0 0, italics added).

In all probability Paul is speaking here about his rebuke to the church (1Co 5:1–13) for allowing a case of incest to go unjudged. Second Corinthians 7:12 seems to refer to this case, which the Corinthians have now apparently dealt with as Paul desired.

But whatever the precise reference, one thing is clear: *New Testament repentance is not confined to the unsaved or to the moment of conversion.* It may take place repeatedly within Christian experience, whenever there is a need for it.

Perhaps it is not too surprising, therefore, that both Martin Luther and John Calvin, the great Reformers, perceived repentance to be a way of summarizing Christian experience.

Luther wrote: "Our Lord and Master Jesus Christ, in saying 'Repent ye, etc.,' willed that the whole life of believers should be repentance."[1] And in a striking passage from the *Institutes*, Calvin says: "In one word I apprehend repentance to be regeneration, the end of which is the restoration of the Divine image within us."[2] Shortly thereafter, the Reformer states:

> Wherefore, in this regeneration, we are restored by the grace of Christ to the righteousness of God, from which we fell in Adam. . . . And this restoration is not accomplished in a single moment, or day, or year.[3]

And he adds that the Lord renews His people's senses to purity so that "they may employ their whole life in the exercise of repentance, and know that this warfare will be terminated only by death."[4]

These observations are extremely valuable, and we will return to them later in this chapter. But just now we must also point out that neither Calvin nor Luther treated repentance as a *condition* for eternal salvation.[5] Both stood firmly for the great Reformation insight expressed in the words *sola fide*—"faith alone."

No other position is biblical or truly evangelical. Faith alone (not repentance *and* faith) is the sole condition for justification and eternal life.

Of all the New Testament writers, Luke speaks the most frequently about repentance. Yet, in one of Luke's most famous stories, a badly shaken Philippian jailer inquires of Paul and Silas, "Sirs, what must I do to be saved?" The answer they give to him is the only answer the Bible knows to such a question: "Believe on the Lord Jesus Christ, and you will be saved, you and your household" (Ac 16:31). There is not a word here—not a syllable!—about repentance. Paul and Silas did *not* say, "Repent and believe," but simply, "believe."

Lordship salvation teachers are in dire straits with a text like this. They are reduced to trying to extract their doctrine from this passage by way of implication.[6] But it is not there, and no amount of theological casuistry can put it there.

As we have already seen, the effort to find the concept of

repentance and surrender in the word "believe" is totally without linguistic foundation. The word "believe" means "believe"—both in English and in Greek.

Indeed, John Calvin long ago rejected the notion that repentance and faith could be identified. He wrote:

> For to include faith in repentance, is repugnant to what Paul says in Acts [20:21]—that he testified "both to the Jews, and also to the Greeks, repentance toward God, and faith toward our Lord Jesus Christ;" where he mentions faith and repentance, as two things totally distinct.[7]

It is an extremely serious matter when the biblical distinction between faith and repentance is collapsed and when repentance is thus made a condition for eternal life. For under this perception of things the New Testament doctrine of faith is radically rewritten and held hostage to the demand for repentance. No wonder that one scholar in the writings of Calvin has been moved to assert:

> Those who teach that repentance precedes faith, and make faith and forgiveness conditional upon repentance, fail to see that theirs is a position parallel to the Roman doctrine of penance which Calvin so strongly opposed.[8]

There can be no compromise on this point if we wish to preserve and to proclaim the biblical truth of *sola fide*. To make repentance a condition for eternal salvation is nothing less than a regression toward Roman Catholic dogma.

"But," someone will say, "does not the Bible also declare God's demand for repentance?" Indeed it does, and perhaps nowhere more forcefully than in Acts 17:30 where Paul declares: "And these times of ignorance God overlooked, but now commands *all men everywhere to repent*"(italics added).

Can this declaration be harmonized with *sola fide*—"faith alone"? Yes, it can, since the Bible is never internally contradictory. And the harmonization is really very easy and natural. How?

Simply put, we may say this: the call to faith represents the call to eternal salvation. The call to repentance is the call to enter into harmonious relations with God.

If the issue is simply, "What must I do to be saved?" the answer is to believe on the Lord Jesus Christ (Ac 16:31). If the issue is the broader one, "How can I get on harmonious terms with God?" the answer is "repentance toward God and faith toward our Lord Jesus Christ" (Ac 20:21).

Moreover, if a person is ready for faith—as the Philippian jailer was—that person can take this step immediately. Thereafter they can be taught what things they need to repent of if they are to walk with God. Along the course of Christian life, the believer will need to repent many times as the Scriptures clearly attest. But no one will be saved more than once.

Thus, though genuine repentance *may* precede salvation (as we shall see), it *need not* do so. And because it is not essential to the saving transaction as such, it is in no sense a condition for that transaction. But the fact still remains that God demands repentance from all and He conditions their *fellowship with Him* on that.

Let us explore this concept in God's Word.

The Meaning of the Original Words

The main words in the Greek New Testament for repentance are the noun *metanoia* ("repentance") and the verb *metanoeō* ("to repent"). Originally, these Greek words meant to change one's mind. But the standard Greek-English dictionary does not list any New Testament passage where the meaning "to change one's mind" actually occurs.[9]

In general use, the Greek verb and noun had come to be roughly equivalent to the English words "to repent" and "repentance."[10] In the Septuagint, or Greek Old Testament, the Greek verb translates a Hebrew word meaning "to regret," "to repent."[11]

It follows that the translation of these words in our English Bibles is generally satisfactory, and the discussion in this chapter will take that fact for granted.[12]

Repentance and John's Gospel

One of the most striking facts about the doctrine of repentance in the Bible is that this doctrine is totally absent from John's gospel. There is not even so much as one reference to it in John's twenty-one chapters! Yet one lordship writer states: "No evangelism that omits the message of repentance can properly be called the gospel, for sinners cannot come to Jesus Christ apart from a radical change of heart, mind, and will."[13]

This is an astounding statement. Since John's gospel *does* omit the message of repentance, are we to conclude that its gospel is not the biblical gospel after all?

The very idea carries its own refutation. The fourth evangelist explicitly claims to be doing evangelism (John 20:30–31). It is not the theology of the gospel of John that is deficient; it is the theology found in lordship salvation. Indeed, the desperate efforts of lordship teachers to read repentance into the fourth gospel show plainly that they have identified their own fundamental weakness.[14] Clearly, the message of John's gospel is complete and adequate without any reference to repentance whatsoever.

In fact it is even plain that John the evangelist *avoids* the doctrine of repentance at a point where it could have been introduced with ease. The point in question is found in the very first chapter, for it is in this chapter that the fourth evangelist reports a dialogue between John the Baptist and a delegation from the religious leadership of Jerusalem. After listening to John deny that he is either the Christ or Elijah, or "the Prophet," the delegation hears him identify himself as simply a "voice of one crying in the wilderness" (Jn 1:19–23). Exasperated, they pose a new question: "Why then do you baptize if you are not the Christ, nor Elijah, nor the Prophet?" (Jn 1:25).

As everyone who has read Matthew, Mark and Luke knows, John the Baptist preached a "baptism of repentance" (Mk 1:4; Lk 3:3; see Mt 3:11). At this critical moment in his dialogue with this influential delegation of Jews, we expect John to announce the purpose of his baptizing ministry in terms of repentance.

But this he doesn't do. Instead, he simply says:

> I baptize with water, but there stands One among you whom
> you do not know. It is He who, coming after me, is preferred

before me, whose sandal strap I am not worthy to loose (1:26–27).

Not a word—not a syllable—about repentance. And if ever there was a perfect place for the evangelist to inject this theme into his gospel, this is the place.

But his silence is deafening!

Many Bible scholars have thought—no doubt correctly—that the unnamed disciple of John the Baptist who is mentioned in John 1:35–40 was none other than the fourth evangelist himself. But if the evangelist was a personal "pupil" of the Baptist before he attached himself to this new Teacher, his silence on the theme of repentance is made all the more amazing.

The silence of chapter one persists to the very end of the book. The fourth gospel says nothing at all about repentance, much less does it connect repentance in any way with eternal life.

This fact is the death knell for lordship theology. Only a resolute blindness can resist the obvious conclusion: *John did not regard repentance as a condition for eternal life.* If he had, he would have said so. After all, that's what his book is all about: obtaining eternal life (Jn 20:30–31).

Repentance in the Gospel of Luke

In striking contrast to the gospel of John, however, are the two books written by Luke. Out of nearly sixty New Testament occurrences of the noun or verb for repentance, twenty-five are found in either the gospel of Luke or the book of Acts.

Repentance, therefore, is a theme which the third evangelist especially has stressed.

If for the moment we pass over Luke's references to this theme in the preaching of John the Baptist (Lk 3:3, 8; Ac 13:24; 19:4), we come to the first mention of repentance in the ministry of Jesus (Lk 5:32) where the striking charge is found that Jesus *has fellowship* with sinners!

In his narrative Luke tells us that, at Levi's feast for our Lord, the scribes and Pharisees complained to His disciples.

And they said: "Why do you *eat and drink* with tax collectors and sinners?" (Lk 5:30; italics added). But, of course, the charge was really directed at Jesus. Why did *He* eat and drink with such people? The Savior's response is familiar and much loved:

Those who are well do not need a physician, but those who are sick. I have not come to call [= invite] the righteous, but sinners, to repentance (Lk 5:31, 32).

"I am here," says our Lord, "to bring spiritual health to those who are sick with sin. I have come to invite sinners to the banquet of repentance."

That is what repentance is all about. It is all about the sinner finding spiritual health. It is all about the sinner "sitting at the table"—having fellowship—with God.

In thinking of matters this way, it is obvious that this is exactly what Luke's story of the prodigal son is all about as well.

No doubt Luke 15 is the greatest chapter on repentance in the entire New Testament, perhaps in the entire Bible. But here, too, the three parables on repentance spring directly out of a question about Jesus' *table fellowship* with sinners. The opening words of Luke 15 set the stage for our Lord's teaching about repentance:

Then all the tax collectors and the sinners drew near to Him to hear Him. And the Pharisees and scribes murmured, saying, "This man receives sinners *and eats with them*" (Lk 15:1–2; italics added).

"How can this man sit down with people like that?" say the self-righteous religious leaders. "How can He have table fellowship with the dregs of society?"

How? The answer was to be found in the heart of God. Like a loving and generous father, He waited to throw His arms around the returning sinner. But accepting that sinner back was not all the Father had in mind. A banquet of joyous fellowship was also a part of His plan.

And that is the story of the prodigal son. Out in the far country, reduced to desperation by his profligate lifestyle, this young man repents. The prodigal son's repentance is recounted by our Lord in these words:

> And when he came to himself, he said, "How many of my father's hired servants have bread enough and to spare, and I perish with hunger! I will arise and go to my father, and will say to him: Father, I have sinned against heaven and before you, and I am no longer worthy to be called your son. Make me like one of your hired servants" (Lk 15:17–19).

"I want to live at home," the prodigal son is saying to himself, "so I will go back and offer my services to my dad in exchange for room and board." In effect, the young man decided, "I want to repair the breach between me and my dad. Maybe I can put things right with an apology and by working for him."

This was a good decision. But it was flawed. His father was not interested in making the bargain his son was thinking about. His dad was prepared to receive him freely. His love for his prodigal boy was not conditioned on any kind of pledge to serve on the farm. Restoring harmony with his father was going to be ever so much easier than he had imagined.

The story of the prodigal son therefore is *not simply a story about salvation.* It is a story about how a long-separated father and son were reunited. It is a story about a dad who did much more than take his boy back. In fact it is a story about how a father lavished his love on an erring son and sat down with him, in fellowship, at a splendid and joyous banquet.

Unmistakably, the story of the prodigal son is the story of the sinner's restoration to fellowship with God our heavenly Father. But repentance is *always* about that, even when the repenting sinner is *already* a Christian!

Let us reconsider the words of Jesus to the Laodicean Christians:

> As many as I love, I rebuke and chasten. Therefore be zealous *and repent.* Behold, I stand at the door and knock. If anyone hears My voice and opens the door, I will come in to him and *dine with him, and he with Me* (Rev 3:19–20; italics added).

Repentance, dining with Jesus, fellowship—such are the intertwining threads which the Bible uses to weave this tapestry of truth. Harmony—fellowship—between a sinful humanity and a forgiving God must always be based on repentance, just as justification must always be based on faith alone.

To be sure, the prodigal son can represent an unsaved man whose repentance gets him turned in the right direction. Many an unsaved person has found salvation very much like that. Dissatisfied with a wasted earthly life, the unsaved sinner decides to "go home" to God, seeking harmony with his Maker. And though he may at first have the mistaken notion that he must work for God's acceptance, in time he will meet a forgiving Father whose love is utterly unconditional and whose salvation is absolutely free.

But the prodigal son can also represent a Christian who has drifted far away from fellowship with the Father and who likewise decides to "go home." Perhaps the Christian even plans to "make up" for failure by working extra hard for God. But on returning, once again there is the encounter with that same forgiving love first experienced at the moment of salvation—whether that moment was recent, or in the distant past.

It is always the same—whether we are coming to God for the first time or for the hundredth time. The Father is there with open arms and with an open heart.

"Take heed to yourselves," Jesus said to His disciples on one occasion. "If your brother sins against you, rebuke him; and *if he repents*, forgive him. And if he sins against you *seven times in a day*, and *seven times in a day* returns to you, saying, '*I repent*,' you shall forgive him" (Lk 17:3–4; italics added).

And why should the disciples of Jesus do that? Because that is exactly what God does for them—for us—every day!

The story of the prodigal son, therefore, is a story which repeats itself—in principle—over and over again in every Christian's life. It is far from exhausted by our initial experience of harmonious contact with God, and those who limit it to that have not really understood it.

And so the Reformers were basically right. It is essentially

correct to say that "our Lord and Master Jesus Christ . . .
willed that the whole life of believers should be repentance." For without repentance, repeated whenever the
need for it exists, there is no fellowship with God.

Repentance in Acts

In his two-volume work, sometimes referred to as Luke-
Acts, Luke has chosen to stress the theme of harmony
between God and man. But Luke was evidently writing to a
Christian audience as his prologue to Theophilus (Lk 1:1–4)
suggests. His subject matter then is chosen for the benefit of
Christians.

The theme of harmony—fellowship—with God was an
appropriate one for Luke to emphasize, especially to believing readers of the first century. For one of the burning issues
of Luke's day was the question of table fellowship between
Jewish and Gentile Christians. How difficult this issue could
become is clearly reflected in Galatians 2:11–21, where Paul
had to stand alone for the right of Gentiles to eat at the same
table with Jews.

But obviously, if God the Father Himself could have
fellowship with repentant sinners, so could any Jewish
believer. And this could be done even if the repenting sinner
was a Gentile.

Like Cornelius! Indeed, there is a sense in which Cornelius is the "prodigal son" of the book of Acts.

It is important to observe, therefore, that Luke's narrative
about Cornelius plays much the same role in Acts as the
story of the prodigal son plays in Luke. And just as Luke
highlights the prodigal's experience, so he also highlights
the experience of Cornelius. For the story of the prodigal son
is by far the longest of the three parables about repentance in
Luke 15, and it is one of the longest stories in the entire third
gospel. The story about Cornelius is also one of the longest
stories in the book of Acts.

And here, too, we meet the issue of table fellowship.
Indeed, when the apostle Peter went up to Jerusalem after
his encounter with Cornelius, he ran into a firestorm of
criticism. Thus we are told:

And when Peter came up to Jerusalem, those of the circumcision contended with him, saying, "You went in to uncircumcised men *and ate with them!*" (Ac 11:2–3; italics added).

Does this sound familiar? This was precisely the criticism that the scribes and Pharisees made about Jesus Himself. It was also the spirit of the elder brother of the prodigal son. In fact, in the concluding section of our Lord's narrative in Luke 15, the father of the repentant boy goes out to the older brother to invite him to the banquet inside.

But the self-righteous older brother rudely rejects the opportunity for fellowship with his father and with his younger brother. His words are indignant:

Lo these many years I have been serving you; I never transgressed your commandment at any time, and yet you never gave me a young goat that I might make merry with my friends. But as soon as this son of yours came, who has devoured your livelihood with harlots, *you killed the fattened calf for him* (Lk 15:29–30; italics added).

"How could you do this?" the older brother complains sullenly. "How can you have a big party for this profligate brother of mine?"

How? Because God desires fellowship with repenting sinners. And He desires this even if those sinners are Gentiles like Cornelius.

No wonder, then, that when Peter finished his account about God's acceptance of Cornelius and of Cornelius's friends, the critics' mouths were stopped. And so we read:

When they heard these things they became silent; and they glorified God, saying, "Then God has also granted to the Gentiles *repentance to life*" (Ac 11:18; italics added).

"Repentance to [or, unto] life"! Repentance that *led to* life—such was Cornelius's actual experience.

Let these words not be misread. Emphatically they do *not* say, "repentance unto *eternal* life." Instead, they are the reflection of that "coming to life" which is always the end result of repentance whether it be the repentance of a Christian or the repentance of the unsaved.

For even to Christians, Paul could say: "For if you live

according to the flesh, *you will die;* but if you through the Spirit put to death the deeds of the body, *you will live*" (Ro 8:13; italics added).

Or, to put it into the words of the father of the prodigal son, "It was right that we should make merry and be glad, for your brother *was dead and is alive again,* and was lost and is found" (Lk 15:32; italics added).

The truth embodied in this declaration is profound. Whether it is a Christian or a non-Christian who wanders off into sin, such a person is a lost and straying sheep, cut off from the *experience* of real life which can only be "tasted" and enjoyed in the presence of God Himself—in fellowship with Him.[15]

Thus to repent is to rediscover our direction and to experience true "life" in harmony with our Maker. But repentance is not the means by which we acquire *eternal* life. Luke's testimony on this point is crystal clear: "And as many as had been appointed to *eternal* life believed" (Ac 13:48; italics added). Not, let us note, "*repented* and believed." Simply, "believed."

What must I do to be saved? The answer of Paul and Silas is the answer of Luke as well: "Believe on the Lord Jesus Christ, and you will be saved" (Ac 16:31). And for that, repentance is *not* a condition. Indeed, Luke never says that repentance is a condition for salvation any more than John the Evangelist says that it is. Eternal life is by faith alone— *sola fide!*

Of course, Cornelius *was* unsaved when Peter reached his house. But the angel had promised Cornelius that Peter "will tell you words by which you and all your household will be saved" (Ac 11:14). However, when Peter came he did *not* preach repentance. Why? Because Cornelius needed to be saved. He had already repented!

Nothing is more evident than this fact. Cornelius had turned from his paganism to seek the God of Israel. To that end he "gave alms generously to the people, and prayed to God always" (Ac 10:2). This was nothing more nor less than Cornelius's search for God and for harmonious relations with his divine Creator. Thus his prayers were directed toward the discovery of how he might find true peace with the God of Israel. The coming of Peter was *the answer* to those prayers.

This point is made clearly in the words Cornelius himself spoke when the apostle arrived:

> And Cornelius said, "Four days ago I was fasting until this hour; and at the ninth hour I prayed in my house, and behold, a man stood before me in bright clothing, and said, 'Cornelius, *your prayer has been heard,* and your alms are remembered in the sight of God. Send therefore to Joppa and call Simon here, whose surname is Peter'" (Ac 10:30–32; italics added).

"Your prayer has been answered," the messenger announced. "You will hear words by which you and all your household will be saved" (Ac 11:14).

What words were those? They were not words about repentance at all. Instead, they were words about faith. Thus Peter says to the crowd assembled in Cornelius's house: "To Him all the prophets witness that, through His name, *whoever believes in Him* will receive remission of sins" (Ac 10:43; italics added).

The results were instantaneous. No sooner are these words out of Peter's mouth than salvation occurs. The Holy Spirit is poured out on his believing hearers (Ac 10:44).

We have already suggested that Cornelius is the "prodigal son" of the book of Acts, and so he is. Living as he did in the "far country" of gentile paganism, this centurion—like the prodigal—"came to himself." He decided, as it were, to "go home" to the true and living God.

Just as a journey separated the prodigal son from his father's farm, so a "journey" was undertaken by Cornelius as well. This journey took time, but Cornelius traveled it with alms, with prayers, and with fasting. And at the end of the road he made precisely the same discovery that the wayward prodigal boy made: He found a loving Father who accepted him freely and who lavished His love on him by pouring out the gift of His own Holy Spirit. Shortly thereafter, Cornelius was baptized and he had fellowship not only with God but with God's servant Peter, whom he asked "to stay a few days" (Ac 10:48).

Who will deny that many people find Christ in very much

this way? Like the prodigal son, and like Cornelius himself, they awaken one day to their need for God. At that point they repent and begin to seek their Creator.

Perhaps they start going to church. Perhaps they take up prayer and Bible reading. Perhaps they begin to give some of their money to God. Perhaps they try to clean up their lifestyle. Such people are under the drawing and convicting power of God's Holy Spirit. But they are not saved by any of the things they do in their search for God. They are not saved by their repentance.

Instead, in such cases, their repentance gets them on the road back to God. It moves them in the right direction, for it moves them to seek harmony with their Maker. But God must always disclose Himself to such people. And indeed He always does, for the Bible declares, "He is a rewarder of those who diligently seek Him" (Heb 11:6).

Somewhere on the road of our search, God meets the repentant sinner. But God's self-disclosure is always the revelation of His full and unconditional love for us. It is always the disclosure of a loving Father who grants everlasting salvation, to anyone who wants it, on the basis of faith alone.

At the end of the search, therefore, the sinner always confronts the divine *sola fide!*

Ready to Believe

We can see, therefore, how God *can* use repentance to draw men to saving faith in Christ. But He does not *need* to. He may use gratitude instead.

The man born blind who was healed by our Lord (Jn 9) is a classic case in point. Our Lord specifically disassociates this man's condition from any sin on either his or his parents' part (vv. 2–3). Not once in His own interaction with this man does our Lord even intimate that He is concerned about the man's sin. By contrast, the legalistic and unbelieving Pharisees accuse him harshly (v. 34). But when the blind man meets the Savior again, the one and only issue between them is faith: He said to him, "Do you believe in the Son of God?"

(v. 35). The blind man replies: "Who is He, Lord, that I may believe in Him?" (v. 36).

"I only need information," this man is saying. "I am ready to believe if you'll just tell me who that Person is."

Our Lord's answer is revelatory: "You have both seen Him and it is He who is talking with you" (9:37).

The blind man's response is immediate: "And he said, 'Lord, I believe!' And he worshiped Him.'"

It would be a true piece of theological casuistry to find repentance in a story like this. It simply is not there.

Unlike the prodigal son who was drawn back to his father by his own empty life in the far country, the blind man is drawn to Jesus by sheer gratitude. Here was the Man who had opened his eyes. He was as ready to believe as a person can get.

And when someone is ready to believe, they can do so immediately. There is no need to preach repentance to such a person at that point. Like the former blind man, they should be invited to believe right then and there.

But as surely as God can use gratitude to bring us to faith, He can also use fear. Such, in fact, was His method with the Philippian jailer. Terrified by the obvious divine intervention in his prison house, shaken no doubt by his own close brush with death (Ac 16:27–29), the jailer is ready—even eager—to be moved. All he needs to be told, therefore, is to believe.

Or again, God may use inward dissatisfaction—our own inner thirst—to bring us to faith in Christ.

This is what He did with the woman at the well of Sychar, whose life had been scarred by a dissatisfying round of unhappy marriages (Jn 4:17–18). Jesus said to her:

> If you knew the gift of God, and who it is who says to you, "Give Me a drink," you would have asked Him, and He would have given you living water (Jn 4:10).

"You are thirsty," Jesus is saying. "So much so, in fact, that if you only knew who I am and the kind of water I can give you, you would already have requested it. That's how thirsty you are!"

Not a word to this woman—not a syllable!—about repentance. She is not even asked to leave her present illicit relationship (Jn 4:18). Why? Didn't Jesus care about that? *Of course* He cared about how she lived. But that was not the issue at that specific time. The issue right then was eternal life.

Repentance could come later—for this woman, for the Philippian jailer, and for the man born blind. If they were to experience *fellowship* with their heavenly Father, it would have to come—not once, but many times. Repentance was indispensable to effective Christian living.

But it was not a condition for eternal life.

We must beware of trying to confine God to a "box" of our own devising. To be sure, God saves every man and woman in the same way—by faith alone. But His methods for bringing people to the moment of faith are rich and varied.

God *may* use repentance. But He may also use gratitude, or fear, or dissatisfaction, or any number of other powerful incentives. God is sovereign. He works with each soul precisely as His own wisdom ordains. But the words of invitation stand irrevocably true: "Whoever desires, let him take the water of life freely" (Rev 22:17).

God has only *one way* of giving this water. He gives it freely. But God has *many ways* of making people want the water He gives.

Other Passages on Repentance

If we will keep carefully in mind the things we have considered thus far, we will be able to understand many other biblical statements about repentance, and thus avoid much confusion and error.

The call to repentance is the call to harmonious relations with God. And that is precisely what it was when John the Baptist preached repentance to Israel (Mt 3:2, 8, 11; Mk 1:4; Lk 3:3, 8). It was a call to the nation to repair its relationship with the God who had selected them out of all the families of the earth, to be His people.

In John's preaching, repentance played precisely the role it had in the life of Cornelius. It was designed to prepare the

nation for faith in the Coming One. Paul states this clearly in
Acts 19:

> Then Paul said, "John indeed baptized with the baptism of
> repentance, saying to the people [= Israel] that they should
> believe on Him who would come after him, that is, on Christ
> Jesus" (Ac 19:4).

Here we see once more that repentance and faith are not the
same thing. Rather, repentance was to *prepare* Israel for
faith, exactly as it also prepared Cornelius the Gentile for
faith.

Moreover, many of the threats voiced against unrepentant
Israel have in view the national calamities that would
overtake them if they remained out of harmony with God.
John the Baptist spoke, for example, of the ax of judgment
that was laid at the root of the trees and which would cut
down every fruitless tree so that it could be cast into the fire
(Mt 3:10; Lk 3:9). Yet this should by no means be read as a
threat of eternal damnation, but rather as a warning about the
fiery holocaust which engulfed the nation in A.D. 70 and
resulted in thousands upon thousands of deaths.

This fact should be evident when we closely consider the
additional words which the Baptist spoke:

> His winnowing fan is in His hand, and He will thoroughly
> purge His threshing floor, and gather His wheat into the barn;
> but *He will burn up* the chaff with unquenchable fire (Mt
> 3:12; italics added).

Every farmer in John's audience understood this analogy
perfectly well. Chaff was *completely burned up* by the fires
to which it was consigned. In short, the chaff was
destroyed.[16]

This can only refer to temporal judgment and physical
death. The unsaved are not "burned up"—they are not
"destroyed"—in hell! In that place, the "worm does not die
and the fire is not quenched" (Mk 9:44, 46, 48). But in the
national tragedy of A.D. 70 the physical lives of many
thousands were cut down and destroyed.

To the same effect are the words of Jesus in Luke 13: "but
unless you repent you will all likewise perish" (13:3, 5).

Here the word "perish" is a perfectly good Greek word which can simply mean "die."

And transparently, Jesus is talking about physical death. The "Galileans whose blood Pilate had mingled with their sacrifices" (Lk 13:1) had *died.*The "eighteen on whom the tower in Siloam fell" had been *"killed"* (Lk 13:4; italics added).

"You're going to die, too," says our Lord, "unless you repent." No doubt many of His hearers *did* die in the devastation the Romans brought to Palestine in A.D. 70. But those who repented—who repaired their relationship with God—would survive.

Let there be no mistaking this principle. The end of the road for any unrepentant sinner is death.[17] This is true even if the unrepentant sinner is already saved and certain of his or her destiny in heaven. Apart from repentance the sinning Christian is headed toward an untimely death under the chastening hand of God.

That is what James had in mind when he urged his Christian brethren to turn one another from any sinful path:

> Brethren, if anyone among you should wander from the truth, and someone turns him back, let him know that *he who turns a sinner from the error of his way will save a soul from death* and cover a multitude of sins (Jas 5:19–20; italics added).

"Be concerned," James is saying, "to seek your brother's repentance whenever you see him going astray. When you do that, you can save his life!"[18]

Conclusion

From what we have seen in this chapter, we must conclude that the call to repentance is *broader than* the call to eternal salvation. It is rather a call to *harmony* between the creature and His Creator, a call to *fellowship* between sinful men and women and a forgiving God.

If we keep this fact firmly in mind, we will never make the mistake of thinking that repentance is a condition for eternal salvation.

Thus it will be with full comprehension that we read words like these:

Thus it is written, and thus it was necessary for the Christ to suffer and to rise from the dead the third day, *and that repentance and remission of* sins should be preached *in His name to all nations, beginning at Jerusalem* (Lk 24:46–47; italics added).

This, of course, is the Lucan form of the Great Commission. And like Matthew's expression of this mandate (Mt 28:18–20), it focuses on the *broad call* into a vital experience with God.[19]

In Matthew, that experience is described as *discipleship* to Jesus Christ our Lord (Mt 28:19) and involves obedience to His commands (28:20). In Luke, that experience is presented as the *fellowship with God* into which we enter by means of "repentance and remission of sins." Indeed—not surprisingly—Luke's form of the Commission immediately follows another instance of *table fellowship* between the disciples and their now risen Lord (Lk 24:42–43).

In contrast to Matthew and Luke, however, stands the gospel of John. Whereas Matthew and Luke focus on *the experience* with God into which people are called, John focuses on a more *narrow* topic: how to get eternal life. And since *that* topic was in his mind, John the Evangelist had no need to discuss repentance.

Of course, the words "repentance and remission of sins" (Lk 24:47) are a *summary* statement. They do not express all the details of Luke's theology. Instead, as we have seen, Luke agreed with John that eternal life—eternal salvation—is by faith alone.

But clearly, the words "repentance and remission of sins" are programmatic for the book of Acts. In fact, repentance and remission of sins are at the core of the preaching that is done there. To begin with, John the Baptist's call to Israel to repent is repeated in the opening chapters of Acts (2:38; 3:19; 5:31). As was true also in John's preaching, this repentance was to be expressed in baptism (Ac 2:38).

Especially noteworthy is Acts 5:30–31, which picks up, in

reference to Israel, the theme of Luke (24:47). Thus, speaking to the Jewish leadership, Peter declares:

> The God of our fathers raised up Jesus whom you killed by hanging on a tree. Him God has exalted with His right hand to be Prince and Savior, *to give repentance to Israel and forgiveness of sins*(Ac 5:30–31; italics added).

So the early preaching in Acts, which *begins at Jerusalem* (Lk 24:47), is a repeat of the call made by John the Baptist to Israel to repair their disastrous breach with God. And if matters were serious in John's day, they were far worse now. For now the nation had crucified the One whom God had made both Lord and Christ (Ac 2:36).

In grim reality, the dreadful fires of A.D. 70 were now that much closer to being kindled.

As Israel rejects this call, however, the invitation to "repentance and remission of sins" moves outward "*to all nations*" (Lk 24:47). The book of Acts is our only biblical record of the spread of God's truth into the gentile world.

In his account of this spread, therefore, Luke selects the story of Cornelius as the centerpiece of his narrative. As we have seen, Cornelius was a striking example of repentance, as he is also an example of the forgiveness of sins, which Cornelius received by faith (Ac 10:43–44).

Cornelius, then, is Luke's prototype and model for Gentiles everywhere, to whom Paul would preach "repentance toward God and faith toward our Lord Jesus Christ" (Ac 20:21).

Paul, of course, was Luke's hero. He is the commanding figure of Luke's narrative. And as Paul's sometimes traveling companion, Luke understood Pauline theology as well as anyone ever has. Luke knew, for example, that if Paul were asked what a man must do to be saved, the answer would be simple and direct: "Believe on the Lord Jesus Christ, and you will be saved" (Ac 16:31).

And what about justification? Luke knew that in Pauline theology this, too, was by faith alone. In fact, Luke quotes Paul on this subject in the synagogue at Antioch of Pisidia: "And by Him *everyone who believes is justified from all things* from which you could not be justified by the law of Moses" (Ac 13:39; italics added].

Not a word here—not a syllable!—about repentance. And how utterly like the book of Romans are such words. And why not? The words are Paul's in both places.

But Luke also knew that Paul preached a *broader message.* That message consisted of a call to men—both Jews and Greeks—to enter into vital fellowship with God Himself. And in this broader message, repentance played a prominent role.

In his sterling defense before King Agrippa and the Roman procurator Festus, Paul declares the full scope of his proclamation to men:

> Therefore, King Agrippa, I was not disobedient to the heavenly vision, but declared first to those in Damascus and in Jerusalem, and throughout all the region of Judea, and then to the Gentiles, *that they should repent, turn to God, and do works suitable to repentance* (Ac 26:19–20; italics added).

"I preach holiness," Paul is saying. "I preach the kind of religious experience that turns people to God and produces good works."

But Paul is *not* saying, as lordship theology alleges, that one cannot be saved without repentance or that one cannot go to heaven unless a life of good works is lived. Paul never said *that!* The Bible never says *that.* What Paul and the Bible *do* say is clear:

> But to him who *does not work* but *believes* on Him who justifies the ungodly, *his faith* is counted for righteousness (Ro 4:5; italics added).

Putting this another way, if you could have inquired of Paul what you needed to do to be eternally saved, he simply would have said: "Believe!"

Yes, the Reformers got it right after all. The inspiring insight of Reformation thought is altogether biblical and true: *Sola fide!*

13

JUSTIFIED BY WORKS

13

Justified by Works

As we have just seen, in his inspiring defense before Agrippa, Festus, and an assemblage of notable men at Caesarea, the apostle Paul offered a sweeping summary of his proclamation of God's truth. Here are those words again:

> Therefore, King Agrippa, I was not disobedient to the heavenly vision, but declared first to those in Damascus and in Jerusalem, and throughout all the region of Judea, and then to the Gentiles, *that they should repent, turn to God, and do works suitable to repentance* (Ac 26:19–20; italics added).

That was Paul's ministry in a nutshell. Wherever he went in the Roman world, he called all to live lives that were characterized by repentance and good works. Yet, as we have also seen, Paul did not mean by these words that justification and eternal life were conditioned in any way on repentance itself or on the good works to which repentance led.

But neither did Paul mean, as some suppose, that "works suitable to repentance" are an *inevitable outcome of* repentance. Much less did he mean they were an *inevitable outcome* of saving faith itself. Those who think they see this in the Acts text are looking at a mirage. There is not a syllable of support in this passage for such a view.

On the contrary, it is as plain as it can be that Paul did not assume that repentance alone would in and of itself necessarily issue in the appropriate works. Instead, the exhortation to do such works was a separate and distinct element in his total message. In fact, as we have already noticed, in his instructions to Titus Paul insisted: "This is a faithful saying, and these things I want you to affirm constantly, that those who have believed in God should be careful to maintain good works" (Tit 3:8; italics added).

There is a very real sense in which the entire experience of a born-again believer *ought to be* an experience of maintaining good works. As Paul stated elsewhere, those who have been saved by grace through faith are "created . . . for good works," in which God intends for us to walk (Eph 2:10).

But the same truth may be stated in terms of discipleship. Indeed, according to the Great Commission, to make disciples means "*teaching them* to observe all things" that Christ has commanded (Mt 28:20). Discipleship is therefore a life in which we *learn* to obey our Lord.

And yet again, this truth may be stated in terms of *fellowship* with God and with Christ. The believer who loves his Lord will keep His Lord's commands and will have a rich experience of the self-disclosure of his Savior (Jn 14:21). Jesus promised a person like this that He and His Father would "come to him and make Our home with him" (see vs. 23).

Walking in good works—fellowship with God—discipleship with Jesus Christ. These are a kind of moral and spiritual "trinity" that are really one great reality: the Christian life. That life, to be sure, is entered by means of a gracious divine gift. But the work of a Christian minister is not finished when someone receives this gift. In a sense, the work has only begun.

Like Paul, therefore, the minister of God's truth must constantly affirm that "those who have believed" should "be careful to maintain good works," never ceasing to arouse them to do "works suitable to repentance." This task endures for as long as Christian ministry to them endures.

And it is in performing this task that the faithful minister of the Word properly honors the true lordship of Jesus Christ. For when the lordship of Jesus is manifested in the lives of His disciples, the world will take note of this, God will be glorified, and believers themselves will be *justified by works.* Concerning this kind of justification we will say more shortly.

The Lordship of Jesus

If John 3:16 is the most fruitful of all salvation texts, it is probable that next to it must stand Acts 16:31. We looked at this passage in the last chapter, but we need to consider it again here:

> And he [the Philippian jailer] brought them out and said, "Sirs, what must I do to be saved?" And they said, "Believe on the Lord Jesus Christ, and you will be saved, you and your household" (Ac 16:30–31).

Eternity alone will reveal how many thousands of souls have rested their eternal happiness and well-being on this uncomplicated declaration. Their ranks will certainly include many who appropriated this promise as very young children, as well as countless others who did so at every age of life.

But to hear lordship theology discuss this text is to abandon all traces of simplicity and to wander off into a wasteland of obscurity and confusion. Again, as we have said, there is obviously nothing here at all about repentance. But neither is there anything about surrender, baptism, good works, or any other similar requirement. Faith alone is presented as the sufficient answer to the question of the inquiring jailer. But lordship teachers are not satisfied with this reply as it stands.

Instead of accepting its obvious meaning, therefore, they attempt to extract their own doctrine from the text by way of implication. Thus, for many lordship teachers, justification for their view is found in the fact that Paul and Silas say, "Believe on the LORD Jesus Christ." They then go on to say that the use of the word "Lord" implies submission to His authority when we believe.[1]

This is a serious and unjustifiable error. It involves a well-known linguistic fallacy sometimes called the "illegitimate totality transfer." In this sort of mistake, an idea drawn out of other words, or out of the general context, is wrongly read back into a particular word as part of its meaning.[2] This is what has happened here. The word "Lord" is used by Paul and Silas to identify the Person in whom the jailer should put his faith, but in no way does it affect the meaning of the word "believe."

A simple illustration may make this point clearer. I may say to a friend: "Trust President Bush to take care of this matter." This is obviously not the same thing as saying: "Submit to the authority of President Bush."

But to adopt the linguistic distortion which lordship theology offers us for Acts 16:31, suppose I said to this friend, "Now remember, I said to trust PRESIDENT Bush! That means you must be prepared to submit to his authority. After all, he *is* the PRESIDENT."

My friend would probably laugh at me for offering him such an obviously tortured explanation of my own words. Or he might say: "How was I supposed to know that's what you meant? You didn't say anything about *obeying* President Bush. You just said trust him and I thought that's what you wanted me to do!"

Of course, on the assumption that I knew how to use the English language skillfully, I might have a very good reason for asking my friend to trust PRESIDENT Bush. If he were merely George Bush, American citizen, there might be some question about whether he could be trusted on a really difficult matter. But the title PRESIDENT identifies him as a man with power and resources far beyond my friend's own. The very title is an invitation to trust.

And so is the title "Lord" in Acts 16:31. This is no mere Jewish man whom the Philippian jailer is being asked to believe in for his eternal well-being. Instead, He is the Lord, with all the power and resources which this illustrious title implies. In the realm of salvation, *He* can deliver what it takes to meet the sinner's need.

But to suggest that some kind of personal surrender of the will is a part of the saving transaction in Acts 16:31, is to violently thrust into the text ideas which it does not contain.

Indeed, we may go further. There is no such thing really as "*making* Jesus Lord of our lives." The Scriptures are clear that He *already is Lord,* not only of Christians but of all unsaved people as well!

That is why the apostle Peter could say to his vast audience on the day of Pentecost: "Therefore let all the house of Israel know assuredly that God has made this Jesus, whom you have crucified, both Lord and Christ" (Ac 2:36).

It didn't matter whether anyone believed that fact or not. Jesus Christ was still their Lord. Thus, also, in addressing the as yet unconverted audience in Cornelius's household, Peter says:

> The word which God sent to the children of Israel, preaching peace by Jesus Christ—He is Lord of all (Ac 10:36).

But if He is "Lord of all," how can anyone make Him what He already is?[3]

Of course, those who employ the expression "make Him Lord of your life" are usually trying to say, "Submit to His lordship in your daily lives." And this is good advice, even though only a born-again Christian can truly carry it out.

This fact is at the very core of biblical Christianity. No unsaved sinner can possibly respond appropriately to the lordship of Christ.[4] The capacity to do so is not within one until rebirth. Only at one's new birth does one receive the full range of capabilities needed for Christian submission and obedience. Or, as Peter stated it, only then do believers receive "all things that pertain to life and godliness" (2 Pe 1:3).

Another way of saying this is to remember that the sinner comes to the Savior like a destitute beggar,[5] unable to offer to God even the right kind of submission.

The prodigal son certainly could not do so with his own father. His thought about offering himself to his dad as a "hired servant" revealed the inadequacy of his own perspective. Not only did he not anticipate his dad's unconditional love, but he was thinking of his own role as that of a "wage earner" on his father's farm.

But as soon as he actually meets his dad and is embraced by him, he drops this idea entirely (Lk 15:20–21). His whole perspective on his relationship with his father could not help but be radically transformed by the overwhelming generosity he encountered on his return home. Now—but only now—could he give his father the right kind of loving, grateful submission.

It is one of the illusions of lordship thought that unsaved people can offer to God any kind of submission which He will accept as part of the saving transaction. On the contrary, only the submission of a redeemed heart is fully acceptable to God. But unsaved people have nothing to offer. They are mere beggars casting themselves on the mercy of God.

Such, in fact, is the deep-seated consciousness of God's redeemed people, as is so eloquently expressed in "Rock of Ages," one of the great hymns of the Church:

> Nothing in my hand I bring,
>   Simply to Thy cross I cling;
> Naked, come to Thee for dress;
>   Helpless, look to Thee for grace;
> Foul, I to the fountain fly,
>   Wash me, Savior, or I die!
>   —A. M. Toplady and Thomas Hastings
>   *Rock of Ages*

Any thinking different from this is not New Testament Christianity.

Honoring His Lordship

But although submission to the lordship of Christ is not in any sense a condition for eternal life, it is crucial to the manifestation of that life. Indeed, to live as a disciple is to live under the lordship of our Savior.

This fact is plainly seen, for example, in the Great Commission, which is prefaced by these words: "And Jesus came and spoke to them, saying, 'All authority has been given to Me in heaven and on earth. Go therefore and make disciples . . .'" (Mt 28:18–19). "My lordship," our Lord is saying, "is foundational to your mandate to make disciples. You will operate against the background of my total authority over heaven and earth."

Obviously, this means that the Commission is to be carried out at His command. But it means more than that. It means, as well, that everything which His servants will encounter, wherever they go to make disciples, is likewise under His sovereign control. Nothing, therefore, can happen to them which He does not sovereignly permit. And, in view of His supreme authority, His servants can anticipate ultimate success and final victory.

But that is not all. In the process of fulfilling the Commission, the servants of Christ are to teach others "to observe all things whatever I [Jesus] have commanded you" (Mt 28:20). Thus, the Commission is not only undertaken as a response to the lordship of God's Son, it actually extends the recognition of that lordship by teaching obedience to His commands.

And in the process, as we have seen, people are drawn into deepening fellowship with the Father and with the Son: "He who has My commandments and keeps them, it is he who loves Me. And he who loves Me will be loved by My Father, and I will love him and manifest Myself to him" (Jn 14:21). Or, as He states it soon afterward: "We will come to him and make Our home with him" (14:23).

The result of such an experience on the divine side will be the glory of God: "By this My Father is *glorified*, that you bear much fruit; so you will be My disciples" (Jn 15:8; italics added).

And on the Christian's side, the result will be "friendship" with the Savior. Indeed, this beautiful concept is first expressed very shortly after the words we have just quoted:

> You are *My friends if you do whatever I command you*. No longer do I call you servants, for a servant does not know what his master is doing; but *I have called you friends*, for all things that I have heard from My Father I have made known to you (Jn 15:14–15; italics added).

For the obedient believer, this is a marvelous outcome.

But there is another side as well: the worldward side. It is precisely this friendship with our Lord Jesus Christ, precisely this obedience to His commands, that creates a compelling testimony to the world. Jesus Himself put it this way:

A new commandment I give to you, that you love one another; as I have loved you, that you also love one another. *By this all will know that you are My disciples*, if you have love for one another (Jn 13:34–35; italics added).

Nothing vindicates the reality of our spiritual experience to the world, nothing verifies our connection with Christ more effectively before other people, than our obedience to His commandments and—above all—to His command to love. In fact, this concept of vindication before others is a repeated New Testament theme.

For example, the apostle Peter states this theme in the same splendid passage where he urges us to add all the Christian virtues to our faith (2 Pe 1:3–7). The pinnacle of this spiritual development, he says, is love (1:7). The Christian who possesses these virtues will be fruitful (1:8), but the Christian who lacks them, the apostle warns, "is blind, cannot see afar off, and has forgotten that he was purged from his old sins" (1:9).

The apostle then follows these observations with an exhortation: "Therefore, brethren, be even more diligent to make your calling and election sure, for if you do these things you will never stumble . . ." (1:10).

We should not suppose, as some have done, that Peter regarded the call and election of his *brethren* as "unsure." Indeed, the words "make . . . sure" translate a Greek phrase that can be rendered to "confirm" or to "verify." But Peter cannot mean that the readers need to "confirm" or "verify" these things *to themselves*. A simple reading of his statements in verses 2–4 should dispel a notion like that.

Peter's readers have faith (v. 1, 5), they have been given "all things that pertain to life and godliness" (v. 3), and these things were received "through the knowledge of Him who has called" them (v. 3). The knowledge of God and of Christ is in fact the very sphere where "grace and peace" will "be multiplied" to them (v. 2). And the apostle's final word to them is an exhortation to "*grow* in the grace and knowledge of our Lord and Savior Jesus Christ" (3:18).

No, there is nothing uncertain or unsure about the call and election of Peter's readership, as if they needed this verification themselves. Peter, like all the writers of New Testament epistles, takes for granted that his audience is not only Christian but is perfectly aware of that fact.

Moreover, as we saw earlier in this book, to believe the biblical promises about eternal life is to believe that one *has* eternal life. If one does not believe that he or she *has* eternal life, one does not believe the promises, since the promises assure believers that we do.

It is utterly wrong to imagine that the first generation of Christians, converted under apostolic doctrine, wrestled with the problem of assurance as do so many evangelicals today. If we think that Peter's readers needed some other grounds of personal assurance than the guarantees that Jesus Christ Himself made to them as believers, we do so without a shred of support from the biblical text.

There is not the slightest reason to think that Peter urged his readers to "verify" their call and election because of some inward need for that.[6] On the contrary, Peter must certainly have thought of the fact that a life characterized by these great Christian virtues will carry with it a visible confirmation to all who observe it that these people are truly called and chosen by God.

This, in fact, was a weighty matter that Peter had already addressed in his previous letter:

> Beloved, I beg you as sojourners and pilgrims, abstain from fleshly lusts which war against the soul, having your conduct honorable among the Gentiles, that when they speak against you as evildoers, they may, *by your good works which they observe, glorify God* in the day of visitation (1Pe 2:11, 12; italics added).

Moreover, Peter alludes to the same theme again in 1 Peter 3:15, 16, where he urges his readers to put their accusers to shame by the kind of conduct that sustains a good conscience. The connection of all this with our Lord's own memorable teaching is plain: "Let your light so shine before men, that they may see your good works and *glorify your Father in heaven*" (Mt 5:16; italics added).

But on the topic which today many hold, that by good works we can assure ourselves of our personal salvation, Peter says nothing at all.

No, that is not the point of obedience to God and to Christ. Instead, obedience is what real discipleship is all about. It is an avenue into fellowship with our Maker and Redeemer. And most important of all, it is the means by which we glorify our Father who is in heaven.

This way of honoring the lordship of Jesus can never flow out of uncertainty about MY relationship to Him. It must come—it can only come—from a heart that has embraced God's unmerited favor and has tasted the heavenly gift which is absolutely free.

The hymn writer has caught this spirit perfectly:

> When I survey the wondrous cross,
> On which the Prince of glory died,
> My richest gain I count but loss,
> And pour contempt on all my pride.
>
> Were the whole realm of nature mine,
> That were a present far too small;
> Love so amazing, so divine,
> Demands my soul, my life, my all.
> —Isaac Watts
> *When I Survey the Wondrous Cross*

Conclusion

It was the very truth we have been discussing that James had in mind when he wrote these words:

> Was not Abraham our father *justified by works* when he offered Isaac his son on the altar? Do you see that faith was working together with his works, and by works faith was made perfect? And the Scripture was fulfilled which says, "Abraham believed God, and it was imputed to him for righteousness. *And he was called the friend of God* (Jas 2:21–23; italics added).

"Abraham," James is saying, "came to be called God's friend through his obedience in offering Isaac on the altar. This fulfilled the goal of his original justification by faith long before. He was now justified by works."

Concerning this famous text the great Reformer John Calvin has written the following:

> James does not mean to teach us where the confidence of our salvation should rest—which is the very point on which Paul does insist. So let us avoid the false reasoning which has trapped the sophists, by taking note of the double meaning: to Paul, the word [justification] denotes our *free imputation of righteousness* before the judgment seat of God, to James, *the demonstration of righteousness* from its effects, *in the sight of men*; ... In this latter sense, we may admit without controversy that man is justified by works, just as you might say a man is enriched by the purchase of a large and costly estate, since his wealth, which beforehand he kept out of sight in a strong-box, has become well known.[7]

Obedience to Christ, friendship with God, justification by works before men!

Such is the only route by which the lordship of Jesus Christ can be honored in the lives of those who have been justified before God by faith alone.

14

WHY DO YOU CALL ME GOOD?

14

Why Do You
Call Me Good?

If there is one human failing more than any other which distorts religious experience, it is our deeply engrained tendency to think of ourselves as "good." It is not surprising that when "the tax collectors and the sinners drew near" to Jesus "to hear Him," the Pharisees and scribes were scandalized and offended by this (Lk 15:1–2). In the parable of the prodigal son, these self-righteous men are represented by the elder brother, who refuses his father's entreaties to come in and celebrate the prodigal's return (v. 25–32).

Again, this same self-righteous spirit is reflected in yet another story that Jesus told. In a parable memorable for drawing a telling contrast, our Lord recounts how a Pharisee and a tax collector went up into the temple to pray. The story is introduced by Luke the Evangelist in words which express its intended purpose pointedly: "And He spoke this parable to some who trusted in themselves that they were righteous, and despised others" (Lk 18:9).

There is something intrinsically timeless about the intention of this parable. Indeed, in every age of the church there are religious men and women who think of themselves as righteous and who entertain no doubt on that score. Virtually without exception, these people despise others whom they regard as their moral and spiritual inferiors.

Yet it must not be supposed that in this parable Jesus is thinking only of people who give God no credit for their moral attainments. On the contrary, they may give Him *all* the credit.

Listen to the Pharisee pray:

> God, *I thank You* that I am not like other men—extortioners, unjust, adulterers, or even as this tax collector. I fast twice a week; I give tithes of all that I possess (Lk 18:11–12; italics added).

How remarkable! The Pharisee does *not* declare that his imagined righteousness was of his own making. Rather, he *thanks God* for it. In fact, he thanks God that he is not "bad" like other people.

The Pharisee, of course, was a religious elitist, a breed which continues to flourish right to the present day. He regarded himself as part of a divinely favored "in-group" (the Pharisees themselves), and he is grateful that his own moral stature rises so much above the level of the poor publican who had also come to pray.

But he was mistaken! The Pharisee *was* like other men, corrupt and sinful in his own proud, religious way.

The tax collector, on the other hand, took an attitude of humility and contrition in his prayer to God:

> And the tax collector, standing afar off, would not so much as raise his eyes to heaven, but beat his breast, saying, "God be merciful to me a sinner!" (Lk 18:13).

Our Lord's use of the contrast between these two men of prayer is powerful:

> I tell you, this man went down to his house *justified* rather than the other; for everyone who exalts himself will be abased, and he who humbles himself will be exalted (18:14; italics added).

It is interesting to observe that Jesus uses here the great Pauline word "justified." Interesting, yes, but not surprising. Even Paul himself acknowledged that the gospel he preached was received "by the revelation of Jesus Christ" (Gal 1:11–12). So the doctrine of justification by faith alone, apart from works, is not simply a Pauline construct. In the final analysis, it is the doctrine of Jesus Christ our Lord.

This doctrine is the antidote to one of our most deadly

religious diseases: spiritual elitism and self-righteousness. Indeed, justification through faith alone is necessitated by an inescapable reality: "There is none righteous, no, not one" (Ro 3:10). Or, as Jesus Himself put it, "No one is good but One, that is, God" (Lk 18:19).

Let the statement of our Lord be squarely confronted. Wherever one looks in the world of men and women, in His day or in ours, one finds no mere mortal who is *truly* good. One finds only sinners—some saved, many unsaved. But sinners all, and without exception.

Yet some sinners are like the Pharisee in the temple. They are convinced that they possess a morality that raises them above the level of the herd. They may even ascribe this morality to God, and they may take it as evidence that they are truly born again.

But they are wrong. No amount of personal righteousness can ever assure us of our standing before God. If we think that it can, we are self-deluded. We have forgotten the most basic fact of all about ourselves: we are *not* good. And if we are *not* good, we can never find true assurance in the presumption that somehow or other we are.

Indeed, the very conviction that our personal righteousness could be adequate to rest assurance about our eternal destiny upon it is the clearest of all indications that we have ceased to see ourselves in true biblical perspective. And such blindness is an open gateway to pride, arrogance, and condemnation of others.

What is urgently needed, therefore, in the evangelical church today is a return to the spirit of the praying publican. We need to grasp again the humbling fact that not only at the moment of justification, but also throughout the entirety of our lives, we are sinners who need the mercy of God.

The Rich Young Ruler

Jesus met a man one time who had the spirit displayed by the Pharisee in the temple. Significantly, Luke records the encounter with this man in the same chapter as the parable we have been considering. The story is the famous one about a rich young ruler.

However, between the parable of the Pharisee and the publican (Lk 18:9–14), and the interview with the rich young ruler (18:18–23), Luke interposes a narrative about little children (18:15–17). This narrative itself cannot be ignored. As Luke reports it, the people are bringing their infants to Jesus "that He might touch them," but His disciples object to this (18:15). Jesus, therefore, summons His disciples and administers a memorable rebuke:

> But Jesus called them to Him and said, "Let the little children come to Me, and do not forbid them; for of such is the kingdom of God. Assuredly, I say to you, whoever does not receive the kingdom of God as a little child will by no means enter it" (Lk 18:16–17).

"Your attitude toward little children is misguided," Jesus is saying to His disciples. "It is in fact a childlike spirit which one needs to enter the kingdom of God." This kind of spirit was precisely the one illustrated by the humble publican who cast himself totally on the mercy of God, and went down to his house *justified*. Of course, it was *not* the spirit of the haughty Pharisee, who thanked God for his own morality and rectitude!

Between those two men a great gulf was fixed. One adduced his own good works; the other relied in childlike simplicity on the divine mercy. Paul would have approved of a contrast like that, for he wrote:

> . . . not by works of righteousness which we have done, but *according to His mercy* He saved us, by the washing of regeneration and renewing of the Holy Spirit . . . that *having been justified* by His grace we should become *heirs according to the hope of eternal life* (Tit 3:5, 7; italics added).

But the rich young ruler who now meets our Lord was a total stranger to truth like this. So far was he from possessing the childlike spirit needed to enter God's kingdom that he stands before us like the praying Pharisee, confident of his own morality and goodness. He opens his interview with Jesus like this: "Good Teacher, what shall I do to inherit eternal life?" (Lk 18:18).

Our Lord's reply appears to evade the issue the young man

had just raised. Jesus says to him, "Why do you call Me good? No one is good but One, that is, God" (Lk 18:19).

But that *was* the issue. The rich young ruler could not be given an answer that he could assimilate, unless this issue was settled first. The issue, in fact, was "goodness."

"Are you sure you know what you're doing when you call Me good?" Jesus is asking. "Do you realize that no one is good but God?"

The young ruler did not realize that. Tragically, he thought that he himself was good. Jesus soon draws this perception from the ruler's own lips. Our Lord continues: "You know the commandments: 'Do not commit adultery,' Do not murder,' 'Do not steal,' 'Do not bear false witness,' 'Honor your father and your mother'" (18:20).

The young man's response is easily the most self-righteous boast to be found anywhere in the New Testament. He replies, "All these I have kept from my youth" (18:21). How readily this man might have joined in the prayer of the Pharisee, "God, I thank You that I am not like other men."

But he *was* like other men. He was not the "good" man this boast makes him out to be. Only God was good! This man was selfish. Moreover, there was no hope for him in the law. Paul knew that fact when he declared: "Therefore by the deeds of the law no flesh will be justified in His sight, for by the law is the knowledge of sin" (Ro 3:20).

This young man's heart had not been properly penetrated by the convicting work of the law. Perhaps he had *not* committed adultery or murder. Perhaps he had *not* stolen or perjured himself. But had he honored his father and mother *from his youth*? Had he never disobeyed them? Had he never failed to render to them their due? No young man walks the face of the earth who can make a claim like that.

Any failure collapsed all his claims under the law, as James puts it so forcefully: "For whoever shall keep the whole law, and yet stumble in one point, he is guilty of all (Jas 2:10). The rich young ruler was a lawbreaker no matter what he thought. Therefore, he was not good. The problem was, he didn't know it.

Our Lord's next remark was cryptic: "You still lack one thing" (Lk 18:22). What did this man lack if he was to possess eternal life? No Christian reader of Luke's day was likely to miss the point. What this man really lacked was the childlike spirit needed to enter the kingdom of God (18:17). What he lacked was that full reliance on God's mercy by which alone he could be justified (18:13–14). What he lacked, in a word, was childlike faith.

Yet in our day and time the appalling answer frequently given to this question is that the young man lacked "submission to Christ," or "the willingness to sacrifice all," or something similar.[1] But this conclusion flies directly into the face of the preceding context in Luke, and it dismisses as irrelevant the repeated statements of John's gospel on the theme of eternal life.[2] Both of these mistakes guarantee confusion and misunderstanding.

Of course the young man needed faith in Christ. What else did Jesus' opening words imply? "Why do you call *Me* good? No one is good but One, that is, *God*" (Lk 18:19; italics added). How loudly do these words proclaim, "You need to think seriously about Who I am"!

Of course, Jesus *was* good, because He was *God*. He was, in fact, the Christ, God's Son. And believing *this* truth, the young man would have possessed eternal life (Jn 20:30–31).[3] But the young ruler is not at all ready to comprehend these facts.

Nor is anyone, really, for whom the thought still lingers that he is "good" in God's sight. Jesus therefore sends this man away with words intended to move his heart in the right direction: "Sell all that you have and distribute to the poor, and you will have treasure in heaven; and come, follow Me" (Lk 18:22). Clearly these words are an invitation to discipleship and to immense self-sacrifice. But we must not make them say something they do not say.

Jesus does *not* say, "The one thing you lack is to sell your goods and give to the poor." Neither does He say, "Selling your goods and giving to the poor is the way to acquire eternal life." No, what Jesus does here is more subtle than either of these things. Perhaps we may paraphrase His words like this: "You *do* lack something. What I suggest is that you give up everything to be My disciple and I guarantee you a rich reward in heaven for that."

What a masterstroke this is in our Lord's efforts to penetrate this ruler's self-righteous façade. On the one hand it probes him sharply on the question of his own goodness. And on the other, it pushes him to consider the Person of Christ.

How readily could his remorse at the thought of giving up all his wealth encourage a new self-assessment. Was he *really* good, if he preferred having his own money to relieving the needs of the poor? Was he *really* good if he preferred earthly treasure to heavenly treasure? Or could it be that he was selfish, materialistic, and earthly minded? After all, Jesus had said, "No one is good but One, that is, God."

But another train of thought was now open to him as well. It might have gone like this:

"Who does this man think he is? Does he imagine that I would give up all my wealth for nothing more than a guarantee from him? How can any rabbi ask a man to put that much confidence in his bare word? The only Person I could trust like that is God Himself!

"But wait! Didn't he say, 'Why do you call me good? No one is good but One, that is, God'?

"Could he possibly have been implying that he is *God*? But how could that be, unless (as some say) he is ... the Christ?"

No doubt Jesus knew that this man would turn his back on this call to discipleship, although among His "pupils" there were some who were unsaved (Jn 6:64). But before the rich young ruler would ever consider so drastic a step as this, he would have to come to a higher view of the Person he had so glibly called "good."

Another way to express this is that Jesus knew that for this young man, trust in His Person would have to precede trust in His promise of heavenly reward. But once he had obtained the gift of life, a gift that was absolutely free, the goal of heavenly treasure *could still be reached* by self-denying discipleship to the Son of God.

Such, indeed, was the course that Peter and the rest had chosen (Lk 18:28). And for their self-sacrifice, they would be rewarded many times over in the present life, and in God's kingdom they would receive an appropriate enrichment in their experience of eternal life (Lk 18:29–30). The life they already possessed by faith, could be possessed in the future even "more abundantly" (Jn 10:10).[4]

Did the rich young ruler ever reach the conclusions to which our Lord's words directed him? Did he ever come to saving faith and to devoted discipleship to Jesus Christ? We do not know and must wait until the Lord comes to find out. But according to Mark, Jesus loved this young man (10:21). We have every reason to be hopeful.

The Life of Faith

The rich young ruler, therefore, lacked faith. He lacked faith in this "Good Teacher" as God's Son, the Giver of eternal life. But naturally, then, he also lacked faith in Him as a Guide for living, and as the One who could be trusted for everything even if the ruler himself had nothing.

What the ruler really trusted was his money. In Mark's account of this incident, Jesus makes this fact plain to His disciples: "Children, how hard it is for those who trust in riches to enter the kingdom of God!" (Mk 10:24).[5]

Christian readers who found this story in Matthew or Mark or Luke could learn a great deal from it. Not only were they reminded that we enter God's kingdom by faith, and not by the works of the law, but they were reminded of something else too—a disciple also *lived* by faith.

In other words, Jesus Christ could be trusted for *everything*. One could make any sacrifice for Him, even give away all one's money, and he would not wind up the loser. In the present time there would be His abundant supply (Lk 18:30), and at the end of the earthly road there would be treasure in heaven.

No wonder, then, that the apostle Paul himself described the Christian life as a life of faith. His words are familiar and well-loved:

> I have been crucified with Christ; it is no longer I who live, but Christ lives in me; and the life which I now live in the flesh *I live by faith in the Son of God*, who loved me and gave Himself for me (Gal 2:20; italics added).

His next words, however, urgently need to be heard afresh in the contemporary evangelical church: "I do not set aside the grace of God; for *if righteousness comes by the law, then Christ died in vain*" (Gal 2:21; italics added).

If the rich young ruler really could have earned righteousness by obedience to the law and selling all he had, there would have been no need for the Cross. Christ would have died in vain.

But for Paul, the death of Christ was not merely essential. It was the starting point for everything. Not only did it mean the end of every effort to secure acceptance before God by the law, but it meant a new kind of experience—a new type of life. Indeed, he wrote: "For I through the law died to the law that I might *live to God*" (Gal 2:19; italics added).

The law was no longer a functioning principle by which Paul lived. He had died to the legalistic way of life, and by faith found a righteousness from God that was apart from the law. But the justifying faith, which ended his relationship to the law, had also united him with the death of Christ. The Cross became the starting point of a new way of living to God. Paul now lived by faith in God's Son.

A life lived that way required continuing reliance on the power and sufficiency of the Lord Jesus Christ. The rich young ruler was not ready for a life like that, but the born-again disciples of the Son of God were.

Conclusion

Some have thought that Paul and the rich young ruler were the same person. It is not possible to either prove or disprove this theory. But so far as their scriptural portraits are concerned, they are not the same person.

The rich young ruler was a man who clung to the illusion that, under the law, he was "good." Paul was a man who had thrown that illusion away and accepted "the righteousness of God" which is "by faith in Jesus Christ" (Ro 3:22; see Php 3:7–9).

The rich young ruler turned his back on the sacrificial path which led to treasure in heaven, while Paul walked that path for many years and could anticipate triumphantly "the crown of righteousness" which the Lord would give him in a day to come (2 Ti 4:8).

The result of their fundamental differences was that Paul had a living Lord on whom he could rely. The rich young ruler had only his money.

15

OUR LIVING LORD

15

Our Living Lord

The earliest Christian churches were like tiny islands surrounded by a sea of pagan religion. Yet these believers made a spectacular claim: Jesus of Nazareth, who had died on a Roman cross, was alive—and He was Lord of all!

Obviously, in a world where there were "many gods and many lords" (1Co 8:5), this was a bold confession to make. But this truth brought courage and power to those who had found eternal life through faith. Very simply it meant that the Jesus they trusted for God's free gift possessed "all authority . . . in heaven and on earth" (Mt 28:18).

And that in turn meant that they could come to Him for anything they needed.

Indeed, the members of the earliest churches were described as people who "called on the name of the Lord." The Greek word for "called on" could indicate a call for help and assistance and, in a legal setting, it could mean "to appeal" (Ac 25:11–12, 21, 25, etc.). Thus, in addressing the Corinthian church in his first epistle to them, Paul writes:

> To the church of God which is at Corinth, to those who are sanctified in Christ Jesus, called to be saints, *with all who in every place call on the name of Jesus Christ our Lord*, both theirs and ours (1Co 1:2; italics added).

The members of the Corinthian church were people who were "washed," "sanctified," and "justified in the name of the Lord Jesus" (1Co 6:11), and they shared this privileged status with believers all over the Roman world who gathered as they did for worship and to invoke the aid and assistance of the risen Christ. In every place where Christians met, they *called on the name of the Lord.*

In fact, this very designation is used to describe the Christian disciples in Acts. In Ananias's prayer to the Lord, he notes that the Saul he is being sent to see "has authority from the chief priests to bind all *who call on Your name*" (Ac 9:14), and those who heard Saul preaching Christ in Jerusalem "were amazed, and said, 'Is this not he who destroyed those *who called on this name in Jerusalem*?'" (9:21).

In his last epistle to Timothy, the apostle urges him to "flee . . . youthful lusts" and to "pursue righteousness, faith, love, peace with those *who call on the Lord* out of a pure heart" (2Ti 2:22). And using a similar expression, the apostle Peter writes, "And if you *call on the Father* . . . conduct yourselves throughout the time of your sojourning here in fear" (1Pe 1:17).

One can scarcely overestimate the immense significance that "calling on the name of the Lord" had for the earliest Christians. All the more so since the term "Lord" was used of the Roman emperor and because those who had the special privilege of Roman citizenship could "call on" him for legal justice and redress. It was precisely this privilege which Paul himself resorted to in the face of the judicial unfairness of the Roman procurator, Festus. The exchange between them is highly charged:

> But Festus, wanting to do the Jews a favor, answered Paul and said, "Are you willing to go up to Jerusalem and there be judged before me concerning these things?"
>
> Then Paul said, "I stand at Caesar's judgment seat, where I ought to be judged. To the Jews I have done no wrong, as you very well know . . . I *appeal to Caesar*" (Ac 25:9–11; italics added).

But the word "appeal" which Paul uses here is the very one that is employed in the New Testament phrase "*call on* the name of the Lord."

Not all Christians held Roman citizenship as Paul did. That privilege was a limited one in Paul's day. But all

Christians did hold citizenship in heaven, and it was their right to "appeal" to a higher court than Caesar's. Indeed, they could even "call on" the name of *Caesar's* Lord since they worshiped Him who is "Lord of all."

And as they relied on His Name, they were living by faith in God's Son.

Saving the Saved

Naturally, there was a great deal to "call on" the Lord about. Every problem of life, every emergency or danger, every need, every concern, could be brought to Him. And He was Lord. He could save, deliver, defend, provide. It was to this distinctively Christian privilege of calling on the Lord that Paul was referring in Romans 10, when he wrote:

> For the Scripture says, "Whoever believes on Him will not be put to shame." For there is no distinction between Jew and Greek, for *the same Lord over all* is rich to all who *call upon Him.* For "whoever *calls upon the name of the Lord* will be saved" (Ro 10:11–13; italics added).

"There is no need," Paul says, "for anyone who has believed in Christ to be put to shame. It doesn't matter whether you are a Jew or a Gentile, because Jesus is Lord of all and lavishly generous to all who call on Him for aid. In fact, in the words of Scripture itself (Joel 2:32), deliverance is available to all who call upon the Lord for it!"

Many readers of Romans 10 have thought that the text talks about how a person could be saved from hell. But this completely ignores the fact that in the New Testament "calling on the name of the Lord" is a *Christian* activity. It also ignores the precise statements of the Pauline text.

Significantly, immediately after the words we have quoted, Paul writes:

> How then shall they call on Him in whom they have not believed? And how shall they believe in Him of whom they have not heard? And how shall they hear without a preacher? And how shall they preach unless they are sent? (Ro 10:14–15a).

It is clear that we have here a series of steps which, to Paul's mind, are distinct and successive. Rearranging them into their proper temporal sequence, we get this:

(1) Preaching can occur only if first the preacher is sent to do it.

   (2) Hearing can occur only if first the message is preached.

      (3) Believing can occur only if first the message is heard.

         (4) Calling on the name of the Lord can occur only if first a person has believed.

"How then shall they call on Him in whom they have not believed?" Paul asks. How can one invoke the aid and assistance of a Lord in whom he does not believe? Obviously, faith in Christ must precede our effort to obtain His aid and deliverance in daily life.

So the salvation Paul has in mind here is broader in scope than simply salvation from eternal damnation. Instead it embraces the whole range of spiritual and personal deliverances which a risen Lord is able to bestow on those who call upon Him for it.

But this is not to be done in a corner. In fact, the other New Testament references to "calling on the name of the Lord" imply that this activity is associated with the public life and witness of the churches. When Paul came to Damascus with authority to bind all who called on the Lord's name (Ac 9:14), he was not looking for closet Christians! He was looking for those who were publicly identified with that Name.

That is why, immediately before the words we have been talking about in Romans 10, Paul made this declaration:

> But the righteousness of faith speaks in this way . . . But what does it say? "The word is near you, even in your mouth and in your heart" (that is, the word of faith which we preach): that if you confess with your mouth the Lord Jesus and believe in your heart that God has raised Him from the dead, you will be saved (Ro 10:6a, 8–9).

As is well known, this famous statement has been used by many to present "confession" as a coordinate condition with faith for obtaining eternal life. But this error should never be made.

To begin with, if that were the intent of Paul's declaration, it would stand absolutely alone on the pages of the New Testament. Not even Paul himself introduces this idea elsewhere in his thirteen letters.

Worse yet, the gospel of John, which explicitly claims to be written to bring people to eternal life (Jn 20:30–31), never even once lays down "confession" as a condition for that life.

Some have tried to deflect the impact of these observations by claiming that the Pauline statement really only teaches that confession is an inevitable result of salvation. But this explanation is not tenable. This is clear from the following verse: "For with the heart one believes to [Greek, "for"] righteousness, and with the mouth confession is made to [Greek, "for"] salvation" (Ro 10:10).

Not only does this verse not say that confession is the *result* of salvation, it states instead that "salvation" *results from confession*,[1] while "righteousness" *results from faith*!

And here lies the real meaning of the text. By "righteousness" Paul obviously refers to "the righteousness of faith" (v. 6) or, in other words, to the truth of justification by faith (v. 3–4). And, for Paul, confession has *nothing at all to do* with that righteousness. The faith that occurs in the heart is the one and only condition for the imputed righteousness of God.

Paul's position on justification by faith alone is in no way modified or altered by Romans 10:9–10. "Confession" was *not* a part of justification precisely because confession is *not* a condition for the righteousness of God. Faith alone is the condition for that, just as faith alone is the condition for eternal life.

But confession with the mouth *is* a condition for the kind of salvation Paul has in mind here. For, as we have already seen from the verses that follow (v. 11–13), Paul is really thinking about the kind of salvation which is available to the believer in Christ *if* that believer is among those who regularly appeal to the name of the risen Lord.

It follows from this that the confession Paul calls for here is not merely telling my neighbor or close friend about my conversion. It is much more than that. It is my public identification as a member of that circle of people who "call on the name of the Lord." Indeed, to call on Him like this in public prayer is nothing less than a confession with my mouth that "Jesus is Lord." My whole experience of Christian victory and deliverance depends on my willingness to do this. The faith that is in my heart needs to be expressed through my lips!

Here, then, we meet the "saving of the saved." Drawing upon that wonderful flexibility which always marked the Greek words for "salvation," Paul stretches our horizons in a challenging fashion. He preached salvation in its most sweeping sense. Those who had been justified by faith were uniquely positioned to experience God's "deliverance" in their lives. They could dare to number themselves openly among those who called on the name of Jesus Christ, the Lord.

Of course, Paul knew only too well that this did not mean the removal of all problems. What it really meant was victory in and over those problems, as one lived the Christian life by faith in God's Son.

And even when Paul faced impending martyrdom, this confidence did not desert him. And though, at his first hearing, no human help was available to him (2Ti 4:16), still he could say triumphantly: "But the Lord stood with me and strengthened me . . . And I was delivered out of the mouth of the lion" (v. 17).

Yet death was coming, as he knew so well (2Ti 4:6-8), but even that death would be a glorious victory. For by his martyrdom for Christ Paul would be *rescued forever* from the evil against which he had struggled so long:

> And the Lord *will deliver me* from every evil work and preserve me for [or, save me into] His heavenly kingdom. To Him be glory forever and ever. Amen! (2Ti 4:18; italics added).

Such in fact is always the experience of those who "call on the name of the Lord" in faith. Tragedy is turned into triumph, disaster into deliverance, by the powerful lordship of Jesus Christ.

Yes, no matter what the circumstances may be, the Lord Jesus Christ can save the saved!

Confident Living

But Christ can do more than that. He can live so dynamically within His disciples that they can enjoy an experiential realization of His presence. They can *know* that He is actually at work in them. This is more, of course, than knowing that we are saved, although our assurance of eternal life is fundamental to all vital Christian experience. What we are talking about is the result of fellowship with Christ, and it is nothing less than the manifestation in our lives of His indwelling presence and power.

It is thrilling, of course, to have a Lord to call on who is "far above all principality and power and might and dominion, and every name that is named" (Eph 1:21). But it is also thrilling to have this same Lord manifesting Himself in our lives—and to be able to recognize that fact.

Such indeed was the confident persuasion of the apostle Paul as he served the risen Christ. And this confidence comes through powerfully as he closes his second letter to the Corinthian church. In the final chapter of that epistle, he writes this:

> I have told you before, and foretell as if I were present the second time . . . that if I come again I will not spare—since you seek a proof of Christ speaking in me, who is not weak toward you, but mighty in you. For though He was crucified in weakness, yet He lives by the power of God. For we also are weak in Him, but we shall live with Him by the power of God toward you (2Co 13:2–4).

What boldness there is in these words! Yet, at the same time, what humility and dependence.

Paul had critics and enemies in the city of Corinth. The believers there listened to these people more than they should have (2Co 10:7–12; 11:12–15). Even some of his own converts apparently wondered whether Paul could furnish "proof of Christ speaking" in him. But Paul had no doubt that he could do that because of the power of the Lord he served.

True, the Savior had suffered crucifixion in the "weakness" of His self-giving death for men. But He had also risen from the dead, and now He lived by the very "power of God." And though Paul knew that he, too, was weak, yet in fellowship with his Lord he could be strong toward these Corinthian believers: ". . . we shall live with Him by the power of God *toward you*" (13:4; italics added).

Yet Paul is not so arrogant as to suppose that such spiritual confidence was his alone. The Corinthians themselves could likewise enjoy a confidence like this:

> Examine yourselves, whether you are in the faith. Prove yourselves. Do you not know [or, recognize] yourselves that Jesus Christ is in you, unless you are disqualified? (2Co 13:5).

Regrettably, however, these forceful words have been sadly misconstrued. They have been read by some interpreters as though they were a challenge to the Corinthians to find out whether they were really saved or not![2]

This is unthinkable. After twelve chapters in which Paul takes their Christianity for granted, can he only now be asking them to make sure they are born again? The question answers itself.

Let the readers of this book examine 2 Corinthians on their own. They will see clearly how often the apostle affirms in one way or another his conviction that his readers are genuinely Christian. Think, for example, of these words:

> . . . *inasmuch as you are manifestly declared to be an epistle of Christ*, ministered by us, *written* not with ink but *by the Spirit of the living God*, not on tablets of stone but *on tablets of flesh*, that is, *of the heart* (2Co 3:3; italics added).

No indeed! Paul is not saying, "Examine yourselves to see whether you are born again, or justified." He is saying, however, "Take stock and see if you are *in the faith*." But that's a different matter.

Surprisingly, the closest analogy to these words of the apostle is to be found in a statement toward the end of his first letter to this same church. There Paul writes like this: "Watch, stand fast *in the faith*, be brave, be strong" (1Co 16:13; italics added).

Elsewhere Paul speaks of those who are "weak in the faith" (Ro 14:1) and of others who need to be "sound in the faith" (Tit 1:13). Even Peter's words suggest a parallel:

Be sober, be vigilant; because your adversary the devil walks about like a roaring lion, seeking whom he may devour. Resist him, steadfast *in the faith* (1Pe 5:8–9; italics added).

To be "in the faith," therefore, is to be operating and acting within the parameters of our Christian convictions and beliefs, precisely as Paul claims to be doing in the immediately preceding verses. It meant living in a dynamic, faith-oriented connection with Jesus Christ, who Himself was living by the power of God (v. 4).

Paul had confidence that he could demonstrate to the Corinthians that he did live like that—that Christ was indeed speaking in him. But he also thinks they can demonstrate the same thing about their own experience of Christ.

"Take a look at yourselves," he challenges them, "test yourselves. Can you not *recognize yourselves* as people in whom Jesus Christ is very much alive? You most certainly can—unless, however, you are 'disqualified.'"

The word "disqualified" is a significant one for Paul. He used it in his first letter to the Corinthian church when he wrote as follows:

But I discipline my body and bring it into subjection, lest, when I have preached to others, *I myself should become disqualified* (1Co 9:27; italics added).

But in that passage the image of the Christian race, or contest, was prominently in Paul's mind. Here in 2 Corinthians the simple translation "disapproved" is probably to be preferred.

So long as the Corinthians were not living "outside the boundaries of their faith," so long as their lives were not "disapproved" by God, they could indeed discern in their own experience—as Paul did in his—the reality of the indwelling Christ.

If John the Evangelist had written this text, he might well have spoken of "abiding in Christ" and of "Christ abiding in us." He might also have spoken of the fruit that will be the manifestation of God's "approval" on that kind of an experience.

Yet whether John or Paul, or any other New Testament writer, each bears witness to the dynamic reality of a life lived in fellowship with Him who is Lord of all. They fully believe, and teach, that this reality can be richly known and experienced by those who are born again.

The songwriter has captured it well:

> Once far from God and dead in sin,
>   No light my heart could see;
> But in God's Word the light I found,
>   Now Christ liveth in me.
> Christ liveth in me, Christ liveth in me,
>   Oh! What a salvation this, that Christ liveth in me.
> —Maj. D. W. Whittle
> *Christ Liveth in Me*

Conclusion

Christ lives in me! What a marvelous conviction to possess! What an excellent experience to live out!

But however rich and deep, however full and fruitful our realization of this privilege may become, it began for all of us in exactly the same way. It began with a simple childlike act of faith. It began with a single, irreversible appropriation of the water of life.

It never started for anyone any other way, and it never will. For the words of our living and all-powerful Lord stand as an authoritative and immutable testimony to God's gracious way of salvation: "Most assuredly, I say to you, he who believes in Me has everlasting life" (Jn 6:47).

There are no other conditions. There are no hidden clauses or commitments. Whoever *wants* it, can have it. The Spirit and the bride themselves say so:

"Whoever desires, let him take the water of life freely" (Rev 22:17).

The chorus writer was correct after all. He breathed the spirit of the Bible when he penned these words:

> Absolutely free! Yes, it is
>   absolutely free!
> For God has given salvation,
>   absolutely free!
> Absolutely free! Yes, it is
>   absolutely free!
> For God has given His great salvation,
>   absolutely free!
>   —Author unknown

Notes

(After the first reference to an author's work, later references to the same work often use a shortened form and the reader is referred back to the initial reference for full bibliographic details.)

Chapter 1

[1] Amazingly, one writer says, "The prodigal who began by demanding an early inheritance was now willing to serve his father as a bond servant. He had made a complete turnaround. His demeanor was one of unconditional surrender, a complete resignation of self and absolute submission to his father. That is the essence of saving faith." John F. MacArthur, Jr., *The Gospel According to Jesus* (Grand Rapids: Academie Books, Zondervan Publishing House, 1988), p. 153.

Note: All further references to the work just cited are simply given as "MacArthur" followed by a page citation at the appropriate point.

[2] MacArthur (p. 23) writes: "Genuine assurance comes from seeing the Holy Spirit's transforming work in one's life, not from clinging to the memory of some experience." Like many statements in MacArthur's book, this is a false antithesis. The proper contrast is not with "the memory of some experience," but with "the promises of God's Word." The New Testament grounds our assurance of salvation on the promises God makes to the believer in His Word and *not* on the transforming work of God's Spirit in our lives. The work of God's Spirit in our lives is in fact an outgrowth of the assurance of salvation and not the basis for that assurance.

[3] In addition to MacArthur's book, already cited, contemporary lordship salvation writings include: James Montgomery Boice, *Christ's Call to Discipleship* (Chicago: Moody Press, 1986), Walter Chantry, *Today's Gospel: Authentic or Synthetic?* (Carlisle, Pa.: The Banner of Truth Trust, 1970), and J. I. Packer, *Evangelism and the Sovereignty of God* (London: Inter-Varsity, 1961).

[4] It is very inaccurate and unfair for MacArthur to say, "This willingness to accommodate so-called carnal Christians has driven some contemporary teachers to define the terms of salvation so loosely that virtually every profession of faith in Christ is regarded as the real thing" (p. 97). A footnote refers to a review of my book, *The Gospel Under Siege* (Dallas: Redención Viva, 1981). MacAr-

205

thur has apparently not read my chapter "False Professors" in *Grace in Eclipse* (Dallas: Redención Viva, 1985; 2nd ed., 1987), although he includes this book in his bibliography (p. 240)!

[5]One should notice the recent agreement reached by some Roman Catholic and Lutheran theologians in the volume entitled, *Justification by Faith: Lutherans and Catholics in Dialogue* VII, ed. H. George Anderson, T. Austin Murphy, and Joseph A. Burgess (Minneapolis: Augsburg, 1985). This agreement has been pointedly criticized by W. Robert Godfrey, "Reversing the Reformation," *Eternity* 35 (Sept. 1984): 26–28; and by C. M. Gullerod, "U.S. Lutheran–Roman Catholic Dialogue on Justification by Faith: An Examination," *Journal of Theology* 24 (1984): 19–24.

Chapter 2

[1]This radical redefinition of saving faith is illustrated by such statements as these from MacArthur:

"Forsaking oneself for Christ's sake is not an optional step of discipleship subsequent to conversion: it is the *sine qua non* of saving faith" (p. 135).

"He is glad to give up all for the kingdom. That is the nature of saving faith" (p. 139).

"His demeanor was one of unconditional surrender, a complete resignation of self and absolute submission to his father. That is the essence of saving faith" (p. 153).

"A concept of faith that excludes obedience corrupts the message of salvation" (p. 174).

"So-called 'faith' in God that does not produce this yearning to submit to His will is not faith at all. The state of mind that refuses obedience is pure and simple unbelief" (p. 176).

Not one of these statements is a true reflection of the biblical doctrine of saving faith. What these claims in fact reveal is a deep-seated fear of the total freeness of God's saving grace, as though that freeness subverted morality. On the contrary, it is precisely the wondrous unconditional love of God that is the root and cause of all New Testament holiness.

[2]This view is often based on a certain way of understanding James 2:14–26. That passage will be considered in a couple of places later in this book, but for a full, documented treatment, see Zane C. Hodges, *Dead Faith—What Is It? A Study of James 2:14–26* (Dallas: Redención Viva, 1987). Likewise the statement "Therefore by their fruits you will know them" (Mt 7:20), is often cited in

this connection. But Matthew 7:15–20 has nothing to do with the faith-works issue, as a comparison with Matthew 12:33–37 makes clear. Matthew 7:15–20 really teaches that false prophets are to be detected *by their words!* For a discussion, see Zane C. Hodges, *Grace in Eclipse*, 2nd ed. (Dallas: Redención Viva, 1987), pp. 14–15.

³Gordon Clark has effectively addressed the absurd distinctions that are often made between ordinary faith and "saving" faith. See his volume *Faith and Saving Faith* (Jefferson, Md.: Trinity Foundation, 1983).

⁴The simplest way for the reader to verify the claim we make in the text is to consult the entry under *pisteuō* ("I believe") found in the standard Greek-English lexicon. See *A Greek-English Lexicon of the New Testament and Other Early Christian Literature: A translation and adaptation of the fourth revised and augmented edition of Walter Bauer's Griechisch-Deutsches Wörterbuch zu den Schriften des Neuen Testaments und der übrigen urchristlichen Literatur* by William F. Arndt and F. Wilbur Gingrich, 2nd edition revised and augmented by F. Wilbur Gingrich and Frederick W. Danker from Walter Bauer's fifth edition, 1958 (Chicago and London: The University of Chicago Press, 1979), pp. 660ff. See also the excellent treatment in Richard W. Christianson, "The Soteriological Significance of Pisteuō in the Gospel of John," Th.M. thesis, Grace Theological Seminary in Winona Lake, Ind., December 1987.

⁵MacArthur seriously distorts a well-known theological definition of faith when he writes, "Berkhof sees three elements to genuine faith: An intellectual element (*notitia*), which is the understanding of truth; an emotional element (*assensus*), which is the conviction and affirmation of truth; and a volitional element (*fiducia*), which is the determination of the will to obey the truth" (p. 173). This is astoundingly inaccurate. *Assensus* is *not* an "emotional element," and *fiducia* means trust and *not* "a determination to obey the truth."

⁶See the artificial and inaccurate application of these terms to the definition of faith as found in the quotation from MacArthur cited in the previous footnote.

⁷R. T. Kendall has nicely summarized John Calvin's own doctrine of saving faith. He writes:

> The position which Calvin wants pre-eminently to establish (and fundamentally assumes) is that faith is *knowledge*. Calvin notes some biblical synonyms for faith, all simple nouns, such

as "recognition" (*agnitio*) and "knowledge" (*scientia*). He describes faith as illumination (*illuminatio*), knowledge as opposed to the submission of our feeling (*cognitio, non sensus nostri submissio*), certainty (*certitudino*), a firm conviction (*solida persuasio*), assurance (*securitas*), firm assurance (*solida securitas*), and full assurance (*plena securitas*).

What stands out in these descriptions is the given, intellectual, passive, and assuring nature of faith. What is absent is a need for gathering faith, voluntarism, faith as man's act, and faith that must await experimental knowledge to verify its presence. Faith is "something merely passive, bringing nothing of ours to the recovering of God's favour but receiving from Christ that which we lack."

This quotation, as well as the references in Calvin's *Institutes* for each point mentioned, is to be found in R. T. Kendall, *Calvin and English Calvinism to 1649* (Oxford: University Press, 1979), p. 19.

[8] The change from John Calvin's view of faith to the view we encounter so frequently in post-Reformation Calvinism has been effectively analyzed by R. T. Kendall (see the work cited in the previous footnote) and by M. Charles Bell, *Calvin and Scottish Theology: The Doctrine of Assurance* (Edinburgh: Handsel, 1985). Kendall's book is his D. Phil. thesis presented at Oxford in 1976 under the title, "The Nature of Saving Faith from William Perkins (d. 1602) to the Westminster Assembly (1643–1649)." See Kendall, p. vii. Bell's book is a revision of his doctoral dissertation done for the University of Aberdeen in 1982. See Bell, p. 4.

[9] This is practically admitted by MacArthur (p. 98). His second appendix ("The Gospel According to Historic Christianity," pp. 221–37), relies heavily on Puritan theologians. But MacArthur seems unaware of the current literature, which has demonstrated that Puritan theology, especially in the area of faith and assurance, did not at all reflect the doctrine of John Calvin himself and is a distinct departure from Reformation thought. See Kendall and Bell in the two previous footnotes.

It is also worth observing that the Reformed theologian Robert L. Dabney pointed out long ago (1890) that he and his fellow Reformed theologians rejected the view of Calvin and Luther that assurance was of the essence of saving faith. That is, Dabney denied that assurance of salvation was an essential part of what it meant to believe in Christ for salvation. He states, "The source of this error [about faith and assurance] is no doubt that doctrine concerning faith which the first Reformers, as Luther and Calvin, were led to adopt . . . ."

Later he also says:

It is very obvious to the attentive reader that these views of faith and assurance which we have examined ground themselves in the faulty definitions of saving faith which we received from the first Reformers. They, as we saw, defined saving faith as a belief that "Christ has saved *me*," making the assurance of hope of its necessary essence. Now, the later Reformers, and those learned, holy and modest teachers of the Reformed Churches . . . have subjected this view to searching examination, and rejected it (as does the Westminster Assembly) on scriptural grounds.

See "Theology of the Plymouth Brethren," in *Discussions by Robert L. Dabney, D.D., LL.D., Professor of Moral Philosophy in the University of Texas, and for Many Years Professor of Theology in Union Theological Seminary in Virginia*, ed. C. R. Vaughan, vol. 1: *Theological and Evangelical* (Richmond, Va.: Presbyterian Committee of Publication, 1890), pp. 173, 183.

Let it be said clearly: *lordship salvation holds a doctrine of saving faith that is in conflict with that of Luther and Calvin and, most importantly, in conflict with God's Word.*

Chapter 3

[1] The woman's reluctance to be too assertive with the men of the village (who held her in low esteem) is reflected by the Greek grammar of her question. This is a case in which "the meaning of [the Greek negative] . . . is slightly modified . . . 4:29 . . . 'that must be the Messiah at last, perhaps this is the Messiah.' " F. Blass and A. Debrunner, *A Greek Grammar of the New Testament and Other Early Christian Literature*, a translation and revision of the ninth/tenth German edition incorporating supplementary notes of A. Debrunner, by Robert W. Funk (Chicago: University of Chicago Press, 1961), p. 221.

[2] Raymond Brown's remarks on 1 John 5:1 are worth noting:

We have seen that all the uses of *pisteuein*, "to believe," in 1 John . . . are christological, either directly (as here) or indirectly. . . . In 5:5b, the next instance of *pisteuein* , the author will speak of the person who "believes that *Jesus* is the Son of God." Thus 5:1 and 5:5 together invoke the full Johannine confession: "Jesus is the Christ, the Son of God" (Jn 20:31). It has been fashionable to affirm that what is demanded is not belief in an intellectual truth about Jesus but belief in a person with whom one enters a relationship. While not denying the latter, I would insist that there is an intellectual content in the Johannine demand for belief, and that one must understand Jesus correctly in order to have a salvific relationship with him.

Raymond E. Brown, *The Epistles of John*, The Anchor Bible (Garden City, N.Y.: Doubleday, 1982), pp. 534–35.

Chapter 4

[1] It is precisely for this reason that John Calvin, for example, held that assurance was of the essence of saving faith. Calvin is emphatic on this point:

> In short, no man is truly a believer, unless he be firmly persuaded, that God is a propitious and benevolent Father to him . . . unless he depend on the promises of the Divine benevolence to him, and feel an undoubted expectation of salvation" (*Institutes* III.II.16).

For additional discussion see Bell, pp. 22–24 (see chap. 2, fn. 8). Note also Dabney's emphatic argument that Calvin held this view, even though Dabney did not: Dabney, pp. 215–18 (see chap. 2, fn. 9).

(Note: Here and elsewhere in this book and in the footnotes, quotations from Calvin's *Institutes of the Christian Religion* are taken from the translation by John Allen in the two-volume edition published at Philadelphia by the Presbyterian Board of Christian Education [n.d.].)

[2] Calvin's splendid definition of saving faith (*Institutes* III.II.7) is worth quoting:

> Now, we shall have a complete definition of faith, if we say, that it is a steady and certain knowledge of the Divine benevolence towards us, which, being founded on the truth of the gratuitous promise in Christ, is both revealed to our minds, and confirmed to our hearts, by the Holy Spirit.

This is light years away from the definition of faith held in lordship salvation. (See the quotations from MacArthur in chap. 2, fn. 1.)

Chapter 5

[1] MacArthur reveals his lack of expertise and understanding when he writes: "The continuing nature of saving faith is underscored by the use of the present tense of the Greek verb *pisteuō* ("believe") throughout the gospel of John [he cites numerous texts in John, Acts and Romans] . . . If believing were a one-time act, the Greek tense in these verses would be aorist" (p. 172).

This is a serious misuse of Greek grammar to affirm a wrong idea. What would MacArthur say if he were told that in Acts 16:31 ("Believe on the Lord Jesus Christ, and you will be saved") the Greek verb is *aorist*, as indeed it is? It is a completely inaccurate concept of the Greek tenses to suggest that the tense itself tells us whether the action is a one-time or a continuing event. One may observe, for example, that in John 6 the author uses several Greek tenses to describe one and the same *single event*—namely, the coming of our Lord from heaven to earth. Thus we read:

6:33 "He who comes down from heaven"
  (present tense)
6:38 "For I have come down from heaven"
  (perfect tense)
6:41 . . . because He said, "I am the bread which came down from heaven"
  (aorist tense)
6:42 ". . . He says, 'I have come down from heaven'"
  (perfect tense)
6:50 "This is the bread which comes down from heaven"
  (present tense)
6:51 "I am the living bread which came down from heaven"
  (aorist tense)
6:58 "This is the bread which came down from heaven"
  (aorist tense)

Obviously, in John 6 we are told nothing about the continuity of the action by the fact that one tense or another is used. Indeed, *three* tenses are used to describe the very same *historical and unrepeated event* of the Incarnation—and the present tense is one of them!

Moreover, in John's gospel, the present participle preceded by the definite article is often used to identify "the one who believes" (or, "he who believes"). The use of the present tense does *not* imply that the action involved cannot stop. On the contrary, the present participle is used of actions that *have* stopped! For example:

Matthew 2:20	*"those who sought* [= article + present participle] . . . are dead"
Mark 5:16	"those who saw it told them how it happened *to him who had been demon-possessed"* (= article + present participle)
Mark 6:14	"John *the Baptist* (= article + present participle) is risen from the dead"
John 9:8	"Is not this *he who sat and begged?"* (= article + two present participles)
Galatians 1:23	*"He who* formerly *persecuted* us" (= article + present participle).

In the final analysis the Greek construction translated by "he who believes" or "the one who believes" is merely descriptive. It identifies a person as "a believer," but it does not specify anything at all about the continuity of the action. We do well to heed Robertson's observation: "But usually the pres. part. is merely descriptive." See A. T. Robertson, *A Grammar of the Greek New Testament in the Light of Historical Research* (Nashville: Broadman, 1934), p. 891.

It follows from what has been said in this note, that it is the context of a statement—and not the tense of the verb—that determines whether the action is viewed as a single act or as a continuing one. As we have pointed out in the text of this chapter, it is clear from the various Johannine contexts that "believing" is viewed as a single act of appropriation.

[2] In an effort to avoid any implication of "easy believism," MacArthur writes about the story in Numbers 21 as follows: "In order to look at the bronze snake on the pole, they had to *drag themselves* to where they could see it. They were in no position to *glance flippantly* at the pole and then *proceed with lives of rebellion"* (p. 46; italics added). Most readers will rightly regard these comments as totally without support from the biblical text in Numbers. MacArthur is guilty of distorting the obvious simplicity of our Lord's illustration about saving faith.

Chapter 6

[1] MacArthur clearly identifies the gospel with the call to discipleship: "The gospel Jesus proclaimed was a call to discipleship . . ." (p. 21); "The call to Calvary must be recognized for what it is: a call to discipleship under the Lordship of Jesus Christ" (p. 30).

But in these statements, as well as throughout the book, MacArthur simply asserts this identification without demonstrating it. Thus he begs the question on a point fundamental to his theology.

[2] The Greek word is *logikon*. The word occurs in secular Greek "meaning 'belonging to speech' and 'belonging to reason', 'rational'. In this latter sense it is found in G[ree]k philosophy, especially the Stoics . . ." See *The New International Dictionary of New Testament Theology*, ed. Colin Brown (Grand Rapids: Zondervan, 1978), 3:1118.

[3] The Lutheran scholar, Anders Nygren, discusses Romans 8:13 very helpfully:

Man can really live only by living "according to the Spirit"; but that means to "put to death the deeds of the body." Here Paul speaks of *"the body,"* where we should have expected him to speak of *"the flesh"* and of putting it to death; for "the flesh" is the antithesis of "the Spirit." In fact it is that antithesis which Paul has in mind. But it is not difficult to see the reasons why he here uses the word "body" and refers to "the deeds of the body." He has just said that the Christian's outward man belongs to the old aeon. The body is subject to death because of sin, even though the spirit is alive because of righteousness. With his "mortal body" the Christian lives in an order where death reigns. *It is here—in his mortal body— that the Christian must carry on his battle against the flesh and death* [italics added]. Here we find additional light on 7:23 where Paul speaks of a "law in his members" which is at war with the law in the Christian's mind. Perhaps we can now see better why Paul longs for deliverance from "this body of death" (7:24).

See Anders Nygren, *Commentary on Romans* (Philadelphia: Fortress, 1949), pp. 326–27.

[4] Lordship salvation cannot escape the charge that it mixes faith and works. The way it does so is succinctly stated by MacArthur: "Obedience is the inevitable manifestation of saving faith" (p. 175).

But this is the same as saying, "Without obedience there is no justification and no heaven." Viewed from *that* standpoint, "obedience" is actually a *condition* for justification and for heaven.

This is *not* an unfair charge. Indeed, it is even admitted by some Reformed theologians. For example, see the claim by Samuel T. Logan that "evangelical obedience is an absolute necessity, a 'condition' in man's justification." Samuel T. Logan, Jr., "The Doctrine of Justification in the Theology of Jonathan Edwards," *Westminster Theological Journal* 46 (1984): 26–52. The quotation just cited is found on p. 43.

Logan argues that faith is both a *cause* and a *condition* for justification, while obedience (= works) is not a *cause* but it IS a *condition* (see pp. 42–48). Precisely this is the position logically necessitated by lordship salvation as well. If heaven really cannot be attained apart from obedience to God—and this is what lordship salvation teaches—then, logically, that obedience is a *condition* for getting there.

There is a distinct lack of candor in the contemporary proclamation of lordship salvation. Why do not lordship teachers simply admit what W. Nicol has frankly stated: "Logically, then, good works must be a condition of justification . . ." and ". . . it is clear that Paul might say: you must do good works, otherwise in the end God will not justify you"? See W. Nicol, "Faith and Works in the Letter of James," in *Essays on the General Epistles of the New Testament*, Neotestamentica 9 (Pretoria: The New Testament Society of South Africa, c1975), p. 22.

In the Pauline passage cited just prior to this footnote reference (Ro 11:6), Paul denies the possibility of intermixing faith and works in the plan of salvation. The "lordship" formulation of the faith/works issue would have been vigorously rejected by Paul. According to the apostle, when works are introduced the character of grace is changed, so that it is no longer grace at all! Works can in no sense be a "condition" of justification. When they are made so, directly or indirectly, Pauline doctrine is abandoned.

Moreover, it is highly misleading for lordship teachers to appeal to the Reformers' insistence that faith and works are always found together (see MacArthur, p. 228). This claim conceals the great gulf that separates the theology of Calvin and Luther from the theology of lordship salvation. As has been pointed out in earlier notes (see chapter 2 note 1 compared with chapter 2 notes 7, 8, and 9 and chapter 4 note 1), lordship theology has abandoned the Reformers' view of the nature of saving faith. It has also shifted the focus and ground of assurance to our works. Thus MacArthur writes:

> Genuine assurance comes from seeing the Holy Spirit's transforming work in one's life, not from clinging to the memory of some experience (p. 23; see chapter 1, note 2).

Calvin's view of this kind of claim is very aptly summarized by Bell, p. 28 (see chap. 2 note 8 for bibliographic data):

> As a general principle, Calvin emphatically warns against looking to ourselves, that is, to our works or the fruit of the Spirit, for certainty of our salvation. We must turn from ourselves to rest solely on the mercy of God. The Scholastics taught that the Christian should look to works and to the virtues of righteousness as proof of salvation. However, Calvin rejects this exhortation to self-examination as a dangerous dogma, and argues that we can never rely on such a subjective basis for assurance, for our sinfulness insures that we will not find peace in this way. Forgetting the judgment of God, we may think ourselves safe when, in fact, we are not. By placing our trust in works, rather than in God's freely given grace, we detract from his salvific work in Jesus Christ. If we look to ourselves, we encounter doubt, which leads to despair, and finally our faith is battered down and blotted out. Arguing that our assurance rests in our union with Christ, Calvin stresses that contemplation of Christ brings assurance of salvation, but self-contemplation is "sure damnation." For this reason, then, our safest course is to look to Christ and distrust ourselves. [For the documentation from Calvin, see Bell's footnotes to the quoted paragraph.]

Clearly, this perspective is diametrically opposed to lordship thought. Any claim lordship teachers might make to represent Reformation doctrine concerning faith and assurance is simply not true.

Finally, we must add that there is no need to quarrel with the Reformers' view that where there is justifying faith, works will undoubtedly exist too. This is a reasonable assumption for any Christian unless he has been converted on his death bed! But it is quite wrong to claim that a life of dedicated obedience is guaranteed by regeneration, or even that such works as there are must be visible to a human observer. God alone may be able to detect the fruits of regeneration in some of His children.

What is wrong in lordship thought is that a life of good works is made the basis of assurance, so that the believer's eyes are distracted from the sufficiency of Christ and His Cross to meet his eternal need. Instead, his eyes are focused on himself. The Reformers understood that there was no assurance in that kind of process at all.

[5] See MacArthur (p. 215): "Paul denounced the notion that the unregenerate can buy merit with God through works." But what follows this statement is barely distinguishable from a "salvation by works" theology. In support of his view of works, MacArthur proceeds to cite Romans 2:6 (God "will render to every man according to his deeds'") and 2:13 ("For not the hearers of the law are just before God, but the doers of the law will be justified").

What conclusion does MacArthur draw from these texts? He states (p. 215): "The saving faith described by the Apostle Paul is a dynamic force that inevitably produces practical righteousness." But this conclusion is *in no way* justified by the quoted texts. Instead, it involves an argumentative fallacy that is commonly found in lordship thought. In fact, it begs the question at a fundamental level.

Neither Romans 2:6 nor 2:13 even remotely imply that faith inevitably produces works. On the contrary, they state as clearly as possible that people will get what they *deserve* from God (2:6) and that *doers* of the law will be justified (2:13)!

What MacArthur has resorted to is the common Reformed method of harmonizing texts like these with the doctrine of justification by faith. This harmonization simply asserts that such texts are intelligible if we realize that faith inevitably produces works. But this is not really an argument at all, but a *petitio principii*: the fallacy of assuming the premise of an argument which one wishes to prove in the conclusion.

The lordship syllogism would be something like this:

Major premise: We are justified by faith.

Minor premise: Faith inevitably produces good works.

Conclusion: We can be judged according to our works.

The "major premise" in this syllogism, of course, is biblical. The minor premise is a theological construct which cannot be established from the Bible. Moreover, the conclusion implicitly contradicts the major premise. If we are saved by faith alone (*sola fide*), how can final judgment be based on works unless works are also a *condition* for justification (see the previous footnote and the discussion there)?

Of course, some lordship theologians will argue that the minor premise is established by James 2. But this is wrong. In the history of the interpretation of James 2:14–26, James's text has *often* been read as teaching that *both* faith *and* works are necessary to final salvation. (See the booklet *Dead Faith—What Is It?* For the bibliographic information, see chap. 2, note 2.) James 2:14–26 does *not* teach, and cannot correctly be made to say, that faith inevitably produces good works. Here, too, lordship theology begs the question by reading into James's text the theological opinion expressed in the minor premise given above.

Moreover, in handling Romans 2:6 and 13, MacArthur forgets that these texts must be read in the light of Paul's exposition in Romans 3 and 4, and especially in light of a statement like this:

> Therefore by the deeds of the law *no flesh will be justified in His sight*, for by the law is the knowledge of sin [Ro 3:20; italics added].

In Romans 2:6 and 13 Paul was stating the *principle* upon which people will be judged in the final judgment. He was certainly *not* affirming that there will actually be people who *are* justified by the law! His point in 2:13 is a warning against thinking that merely hearing the law could be a basis for acceptance before God (as the Jews were tempted to think: Ro 2:17–29). Only "the doers of the law" would be justified. But in Pauline theology, there were no such people (Ro 3:19–20)!

It should be kept in mind that, of course, every unsaved person will have "his day in court." For unsaved people, judgment *will be* according to their works (Rev 20:12). But the result of a judgment by works is a foregone conclusion: condemnation (Rev 20:15).

By contrast there is no such thing as a judgment for the believer to determine whether he goes to heaven or hell. Indeed the verdict of acquittal has already been rendered (justification). And our Lord Himself said:

> Most assuredly, I say to you, he who hears My word and believes in Him who sent Me has everlasting life, and shall not come into judgment, but has passed from death into life (Jn 5:24; italics added).

There is no final judgment at all for the believer if by that we mean a "judicial examination" to determine his eternal destiny. Eternal life is already possessed by the believer as an irrevocable free gift (see chapter 5). Of course, the believer must give an account of his Christian stewardship at the judgment seat of Christ, but that is another matter (Rom 14:10-12). Even if his works are burned, he is still saved! Thus Paul could write:

> If anyone's work which he has built on it endures, he will receive a reward. If anyone's work is burned, he will suffer loss; but *he himself will be saved*, yet so as through fire (1Co 3:14–15; italics added).

The theology of lordship salvation on the subject of faith and works is a hopelessly confused and unbiblical system of thought.

[6]The view is often expressed that Paul's condemnation of works as having no salvific role is really only a condemnation of *legalistic* works—works done to obtain merit before God. (See, for example, MacArthur, p. 215.) But this is really an effort to redefine Pauline theology in order to allow a role for works in the salvific process. It has no basis in Scripture and is ably refuted by Douglas J. Moo, " 'Law,' 'Works of the Law,' and Legalism in Paul," *Westminster Theological Journal* 45 (1983): 73–100. Note this statement in particular:

> First, as we have seen, Paul denies justification through "works" as often as he denies it through "works of the law." "Works" had no more place in the selection of Abraham and Jacob, who bore no relationship to the law . . . than in the justification of Galatian Gentiles, who were being encouraged to supplement their faith with "works of the law." In other words, Paul appears to criticize "works of the law" not because they are *nomou* ("of the law") but because they are *erga* ("works") [pp. 96–97].

[7]MacArthur, p. 31.

Chapter 7

[1]For a treatment of the book of Hebrews which views it as a challenge to Christians to persevere in the faith, see Zane C. Hodges, "Hebrews," in *The Bible Knowledge Commentary*, New Testament edition, eds. John F. Walvoord and Roy B. Zuck (Wheaton, Ill.: Victor Books, 1983), pp. 777–813.

[2]See chapter 5.

[3]See the discussions of this issue in Kendall, pp. 13–18, 29–33, 149–50; and Bell, pp. 13–18. For bibliographic data, see chapter 2, notes 7–8.

Chapter 8

[1]For a discussion of 2 Corinthians 13:5, see chapter 15.

[2]For a perceptive discussion of this problem in contemporary religious life, see Bell, pp. 200–202. (See chapter 2, note 8, for bibliographic data.)

Chapter 9

[1] MacArthur (p. 173) writes: "As a divine gift, faith is neither transient nor impotent. It has an abiding quality that guarantees its endurance to the end."

But none of these claims can be demonstrated from Scripture. MacArthur argues (pp. 172–73) that Ephesians 2:8–9 teach that "the entire process of grace, faith, and salvation" is "the gift of God." This assertion is unfounded. The phrase in 2:8 "and that not of yourselves" can be readily taken as a reference simply to the salvation spoken of here. Moreover, it is inherently contradictory to speak here of "grace" as the "gift of God." The *giving of a gift is an act* of "grace," but "grace," when viewed as a principle or basis of Divine action, is never said to be a "gift," or part of a gift. In the same way, as the story in John 4 shows (see 4:10), the "gift of God" is to be distinguished from "asking for" or "receiving" it. The Bible never affirms that saving faith per se is a gift.

MacArthur has here confused three distinct categories: (1) the gift itself (salvation); (2) the grounds on which the gift is given ("by grace"); and (3) the means by which the gift is received ("through faith"). As all perceptive theologians will recognize, what MacArthur has done is to impose his own theological grid on Ephesians 2:8–9.

Under MacArthur's view, there is no room for human responsibility in the matter of responding to the gospel. God does everything, including the impartation of faith. Indeed, MacArthur apparently holds the Reformed view that regeneration logically *precedes* saving faith. Note his statement on p. 75: "Spiritual sight is a gift from God that *makes one willing and able to believe*" (italics added). Thus "spiritual sight" logically *precedes* faith in MacArthur's theology.

The same theology seems to appear in MacArthur's Preface (p. xiii): "Saving faith, repentance, commitment, and obedience are all divine works, *wrought by the Holy Spirit in the heart of everyone who is saved*" (italics added).

By contrast, in Scripture, *faith* logically precedes *salvation*. Paul and Silas did not say to the Philippian jailer, "Be saved, and you will believe on the Lord Jesus Christ"! They said, "Believe on the Lord Jesus Christ, and you will be saved"!

The theology MacArthur evidently embraces is a formula for despair. The unsaved person (who *could be* nonelect!) is in hopeless straits. He ought really to be told that, if he is indeed not among the elect, there is nothing he can do because God may have decreed never to regenerate him. Thus he cannot truly believe, repent, commit, or obey—since all these things are God's gift to the elect.

But equally, the Christian himself cannot be sure he has the faith of God's elect unless he perseveres to the end. Thus every Christian must live with the possibility that he may prove in the end to be nonelect, that is, "reprobate"!

Of course, these problems arise precisely from the doctrine of "temporary [= false] faith" that has plagued Reformed theology down through the years. For discussions, see Kendall, pp. 6–9, 67–76 (and other references in the index); and Bell, pp. 10–11, 32, 46–47 and passim. For bibliographic data, see chapter 2, notes 7–8.

MacArthur's theological posture is Puritan and Reformed—a very narrow strand of the overall evangelical tradition. The doctrine that divine regeneration is logically prior to saving faith is a view that in no sense deserves to be identified as traditional orthodoxy. It is certainly not biblical.

[2] It is an unjustified dogmatic assertion for MacArthur (p. 33) to write:

> Thus salvation cannot be defective in any dimension. As a part of His saving work, God will produce repentance, faith, sanctification, yieldedness, obedience, and ultimately glorification. Since He is not dependent on human effort in producing those elements, an experience that lacks any of them cannot be the saving work of God.

With these words, lordship theology collapses in on itself to produce a conceptual "black hole." God, we are told, needs no human effort to accomplish His saving work in an individual. Salvation thus cannot be "defective"!

But what is sin in the life of a believer? Is it not a defect? But since God needs no human effort to accomplish His will in the believer, why is there any sin at all? Under the terms expressed by MacArthur, God must be to blame for the sin that remains in the life of a Christian. At the end of this line of theological reasoning lies an unbiblical perfectionism.

Lordship theologians are compelled to answer this objection by saying, in effect, that *some degree of sin* in a believer does not make God's saving work defective, but *a lot of sin* does! But the illogic of this position is evident. *Any and all sin* is a grievous and deplorable defect!

The problem is that lordship teachers have set up their own standards by which to measure God's saving work in an individual life. If these standards are not met, lordship thought insists that God cannot be involved. Only if the professing believer meets the level of attainment required by lordship thinkers—only then will lordship theologians admit that such a believer may be truly saved.

Such an approach to the issue of sin in the believer's life is not only unbiblical, it carries its own condemnation with it. It is a transparent effort to play God.

[3] The statement of 2 Timothy 2:19, "The Lord knows those who are His," means more, of course, than simply that the Lord can identify the people who belong to Him. The Greek word for know (*egnōn* from *ginōskō*) implies in such statements that God "acknowledges" such people as His. The exact opposite of this is found in Matthew 7:23—"I never knew you." (For this use of the Greek verb see the Bauer-Gingrich-Danker lexicon, p. 161, paragraph 7. For bibliographic data about the lexicon, see chapter 2, note 4.)

[4] MacArthur (p. 172) completely misses the gracious tone of 2 Timothy 2:13 when he writes: "Because He is faithful to Himself, *He will condemn them* . . . "(italics added). But the concept of being "faithful to condemn" is totally foreign to, and utterly without analogy in, the New Testament. MacArthur is simply reading his own judgmental theology into one of the most reassuring statements in the Bible.

Chapter 10

[1] See the excellent discussion of Romans 8:12–17 in Anders Nygren, *Commentary on Romans* (Philadelphia: Fortress, 1949), pp. 325–20.

[2] It is probably not surprising that MacArthur (p. 218) calls James 4:7–10 "the most comprehensive invitation to salvation in the epistles." But this comment shows how hopelessly lordship thought has mixed its categories.

James persistently calls his readers "brethren" (1:2, 16, 19; 2:1, 5, 14–15; 3:1, 10, 12; 4:11 [!!]; 5:7, 9–10, 12, 19) and never once calls them to salvation. In the passage MacArthur cites, there is no call to faith at all. Instead, James's Christian brothers are being called to repent of their worldly spirit and behavior.

MacArthur's comment on James 4:7–10 illustrates the enormous capacity of lordship theology to misread and misrepresent the Scriptures.

[3] The statement of Dibelius is worth quoting: "But in all of the instances [in James] which have been examined thus far what is involved is the faith which the Christian has, never the faith of the

sinner which first brings him to God . . . The faith which is mentioned in this section [2:14–26] can be presupposed in every Christian . . . [James's] intention is not dogmatically oriented, but practically oriented: *he wishes to admonish the Christians to practice their faith, i.e., their Christianity, by works.*" Martin Dibelius, *James*, rev. Heinrich Greeven, trans. Michael A. Williams, ed. Helmut Koester, Hermeneia (Philadephia: Fortress, Eng. ed. 1976), p. 178 (italics his).

Chapter 11

[1] It is interesting that John 15:1–8 is not discussed by MacArthur.

[2] It should be noted how often in the Old Testament fire is used as a metaphor for God's *temporal* anger and for the calamities which that anger brings. See, in addition to the references given in the text, Psalms 21:8–10; 97:2–5; Isaiah 5:24–25; 29:5–7; Jeremiah 21:12; Amos 1:4, 7, 10, 12, 14; and many, many other passages too numerous to cite here. It is a mistake to suppose that the metaphorical use of fire as a reference to divine judgment is most naturally taken as a reference to eternal damnation. On the contrary, this biblical metaphor most often refers to God's temporal wrath and retribution. In Christian experience, fire can also be a figure of temporal trials (see 1Pe 1:6–7; 4:12).

Chapter 12

[1] See *Luther's and Zwingli's Propositions for Debate: The Ninety-Five Theses of 31 October 1517 and the Sixty-Seven Articles of 19 January 1523* , in the original version and contemporary translations, with a new English translation, introduction, and bibliography by Carl S. Meyer (Leiden: E. J. Brill, 1963), pp. 2–3.

[2] *Institutes* III.III.9.

[3] Ibid.

[4] Ibid.

[5] Both Reformers treated repentance as a *fruit* of faith. Cf. *Institutes* III.III.1. And note this interesting discussion by Luther:

In the first place, they [the Romanists] teach that contrition takes precedence over, and is far superior to, faith in the promise, as if contrition were not a work of faith, but a merit; indeed, they do not mention faith at all. They stick so closely to works and to those passages of Scripture where we read of many who obtained pardon by reason of their contrition and humility of heart; but they take no account of the faith which effected this contrition and sorrow of heart, as is written of the men of Nineveh in Jon. 3 [:5]: "And the people of Nineveh believed God; they proclaimed a fast, etc." Others again, more bold and wicked, have invented a so-called "attrition," which is converted into contrition by the power of the keys, of which they know nothing. This attrition they grant to the wicked and unbelieving, and thus abolish contrition altogether. O the intolerable wrath of God, that such things should be taught in the church of Christ! Thus, with both faith and its work destroyed, we go on secure in the doctrines and opinions of men, or rather we perish in them. A contrite heart is a precious thing, but it is found only where there is an ardent faith in the promises and threats of God. Such faith, intent on the immutable truth of God, makes the conscience tremble, terrifies it and bruises it; and afterwards, when it is contrite, raises it up, consoles it, and preserves it. Thus the truth of God's threat is the cause of contrition, and the truth of his promise the cause of consolation, if it is believed. By such faith a man "merits" the forgiveness of sins. Therefore faith should be taught and aroused before all else. Once faith is obtained, contrition and consolation will follow inevitably of themselves.

A paragraph later, he adds:

Beware then, of putting your trust in your own contrition and of ascribing the forgiveness of sins to your own remorse. God does not look on you with favor because of that, but because of the faith by which you have believed his threats and promises, and which has effected such sorrow within you. Thus we owe whatever good there may be in our penance, not to our scrupulous enumeration of sins, but to the truth of God and to our faith. All other things are the works and fruits which follow of their own accord. They do not make a man good, but are done by the man who is already made good through faith in the truth of God. Even so, "smoke goes up in his wrath; because he is angry he shakes the mountains and sets them on fire," as it is said in Ps. 18 [:8,7]) [sic]. First comes the terror of this threatening, which sets the wicked on fire, then faith, accepting this, sends up smoke-clouds of contrition, etc.

Martin Luther, "The Babylonian Captivity of the Church," *Luther's Works*, vol. 36: *Word and Sacrament II*, ed. Abdel Ross

Wentz, gen. ed. Helmut T. Lehmann (Philadelphia: Muhlenberg, 1959), pp. 84, 85.

[6]For the idea that the word "Lord" here implies "lordship" doctrine, see our discussion of Acts 16:31 in chapter 13.

[7]*Institutes* III.III.5.

[8]See M. Charles Bell, p. 39 n. 208 (bibliographic data: chap. 2, n. 8).

[9]See the Bauer-Gingrich-Danker lexicon, pp. 511–12 (bibliographic data: chap. 2, n. 4).

[10]The concept of "sorrow" or "remorse" is frequently implied by the English word, though by no means always implied. In this regard, the English context is decisive for the English word, just as the Greek context is for the Greek word. "Remorse" cannot always be presupposed in either English or Greek, so that the idea is often softened to the level of "regret." See the lexicon cited in the previous note.

[11]The Hebrew word is *niḥam.* It is not appropriate to say, as J. Goetzmann does, that "the New Testament does not follow LXX usage but employs *metanoeō* to express the force of *šûḇ,* turn around." (See article on *metanoia,* in *The New International Dictionary of New Testament Theology,* ed. Colin Brown (Grand Rapids: Zondervan, 1975), 1:357. On the contary, the New Testament word for "turning around" is the verb *epistrephō* (noun = *epistrophē*). There is no good reason to think that the Septuagint translators and the New Testament writers did not share the same understanding of *metanoeō* as a functional equivalent to *niḥam.*

[12]Many very fine expositors of the New Testament who preach a completely free salvation hold the view that "to repent" means simply "to change one's mind." They then affirm that in salvation contexts the call to repent means basically nothing more than the change of mind involved in moving from an attitude of unbelief to one of faith in Christ. For such expositors, repentance becomes almost a synonym for faith. Or, at least, it is the opposite side of the coin since some change of mind is necessarily involved in coming to faith. I certainly respect this point of view even if I cannot agree with it. It is a view that maintains the integrity of the gospel offer. For a scholarly discussion from this perspective, see Robert Nicholas Wilkin, *Repentance as a Condition for Salvation in the New Testament* (unpublished Th.D. dissertation, Dallas Theological Seminary, 1985).

[13]MacArthur, p. 167.

[14]Astoundingly, MacArthur finds repentance implied in Nicodemus's questions, "How can a man be born when he is old? Can he

enter a second time into his mother's womb and be born?" (p. 40) and in our Lord's reference to the brazen serpent story of Numbers 21 (p. 46). But in both cases, repentance has scarcely ever been detected in either case in the Johannine narrative. MacArthur's efforts to extract it from John's text will be seen by any fair-minded person to be a counsel of desperation.

15The reader is referred again to Anders Nygren's excellent discussion of Romans 8:12-17 (see chap. 6, n. 3). Particularly appropriate here are these words by Nygren (p. 326):

> So there are two different ways to live. Man can "live according to the flesh" or "live according to the Spirit." As to the former manner of life, it must be said that it is not really life. On the contrary, in its basic nature it is quite the opposite. Therefore, Paul says, "If you live according to the flesh you will *die*" [italics in the original].

Shortly after these words, alluding to Romans 8:10 ("if Christ is in you, the body is dead because of sin"), Nygren writes (p. 327), "With his 'mortal body' the Christian lives in an order where death reigns. It is here—in his mortal body—that the Christian must carry on his battle against the flesh and death." Sin, then, involves an experience that cannot truly be called "life." It is, in fact, a species of "death." All repentance, therefore—whether by the unsaved or the saved—is like an awakening from a state of "death" to an experience of "life" with God.

16The Greek verb for "burn up" is intensive and is normally applied to things which are fully consumed by fire (see Ac 19:19; 1Co 3:15; Heb 13:11; Rev 8:7). Of course, the contextual imagery of chaff makes the force of the verb plain in Matthew 3:12. The same verb is also used in the parallel passage in Luke 3:17. Even in the case of the darnel (= "tares") in Matthew 13:30, 40, the metaphor suggests complete destruction. The reference in Matthew 13 will then be to the eschatological judgments of the end-times, which result in such widespread destruction of life that the extinction of the human race is threatened (Mt 24:22).

The reference to "unquenchable fire" in Matthew 3:12 (and Lk 3:17) means, of course, that the fire is irresistible and cannot be extinguished until the chaff is destroyed. The fires of hell are also unquenchable (Mk 9:44, 46, 48), but they do not *consume*, or "burn up," the lost.

17Of course, if an unrepentant attitude deters a person from seeking or accepting God's free and unconditional salvation, he will not only die but also end in hell. No doubt, the rich man of our Lord's well-known narrative was a case in point (Lk 16:19–31).

But we should not look for theological sophistication in this man who has just awakened in Hades (16:23). He is mistaken about the possibility of receiving relief from Lazarus (16:24–26), and he is also mistaken about the impact Lazarus could have on his five living brothers (16:27–31). But at least he does know that his brothers need to get right with God, and it was natural for him, as a Jew, to indicate this need by a reference to repentance (16:30). But we are certainly not to infer that he awakened in hell with a clear-cut theology of salvation by grace through faith!

[18]Paul is close to James in describing the Corinthians' sorrow and repentance as leading "to salvation [or, deliverance], not to be regretted; but the sorrow of the world produces *death*" (2Co 7:10; italics added). The Corinthians have chosen a life-saving path (see v. 11).

[19]Not surprisingly, the apostle Peter refers to this broader call from God in 2 Peter 3:9 when he writes, "The Lord . . . is longsuffering toward us, not desiring that any should perish but that all should come to repentance." Repentance is God's universal desire for people. Not only does He not wish that any man undergo eternal judgment, but also He wants every man to repent. That is, God desires harmony and fellowship with all, and He desires the damnation of none.

Chapter 13

[1]See MacArthur, pp. 28–29, 207. He states clearly, "No promise of salvation is ever extended to those who refuse to accede to Christ's lordship. Thus, there is no salvation except 'lordship' salvation" (p. 28). On the contrary, the Scripture extends the promise of salvation to "whoever believes in Him" (e.g., John 3:16). Precisely this uncomplicated offer is what lordship teachers deny. Their efforts to evade texts like John 3:16 and Revelation 22:17 ("whoever desires, let him take the water of life freely") is what leads to their unbiblical redefinition of saving faith as more than a simple, childlike act of trust.

[2]For a discussion of "illegitimate totality transfer," see James Barr, *The Semantics of Biblical Language* (Oxford: University Press, 1961), pp. 218–22.

[3]This point is admitted by MacArthur (p. 28).

[4]Lordship thinkers can admit this if they hold that regeneration logically precedes faith and commitment to the lordship of Jesus. (See chap. 9, n. 1.)

[5] In an article of great importance for the current debate over the nature of saving faith, Lutheran theologian Robert D. Preus has aptly referred to the familiar Lutheran formulation that faith is "like the empty hand of a beggar receiving a gift." See Robert D. Preus, "Perennial Problems in the Doctrine of Justification," *Concordia Theological Quarterly* 45 (July 1981): 172.

As over against the Puritan and Reformed view that faith is an act of the will, Preus insists on the traditional Lutheran understanding of faith as "pure receptivity." Thus he writes (p. 171):

> Finally, we must comment briefly about faith in our model. First, and most importantly, it must be considered in the article of justification as pure receptivity. Melanchthon made this point crystal clear in the statements cited above when he consistently used verbs for receptivity (*consequor, apprehendo, accipio*) in describing the place of faith in what our later Lutheran theologians called God's *modus justificationis*. But does not Melanchthon also call justifying faith trust (Apol. IV,48, German text; 337)? Yes, but trust very definitely in that it receives the promises of its appropriate object. And faith as receptivity has the element of trust in it (Apol. IV,48,227). Years later, in defending the confessional understanding of justifying faith, Quenstedt calls it a *fiducialis apprehensio*.

Preus also quotes Martin Luther to the same effect (p. 177, citing WA²XI.1104):

> Faith holds out the hand and the sack and just lets the good be done to it. For as God is the giver who bestows such things in His love, we are the receivers who receive the gift through faith which does nothing. For it is not our doing and cannot be merited by our work. It has already been granted and given. You need only open your mouth, or rather, your heart, and keep still and let yourself be filled.

Calvin, of course, essentially agreed with this view of faith (see chap. 2, n. 7). But lordship theology abandons Reformation thought about the nature of saving faith and thus also abandons biblical thought.

One further section of Preus's article (p. 172) is so pertinent that it deserves quotation:

> At least a century was spent by the greatest Lutheran theologians of the age, attempting to defend and clarify the Lutheran position, so crucial to the understanding of justifi-

cation and communicating the Christian message. Their adversaries were the Romanists who denied that justifying faith was trust and receptivity, but taught that justifying faith was an act of man which could be considered a good work (formed by love); its object was the entire Christian dogma (*fides dogmatica* , Bellarmine). The Arminians too opposed the Lutheran doctrine by making faith (which they granted was trust) a work (*actus*) of man. Like the Romanists they had a synergistic notion of how man came to faith. And, of course, there were the Socinians, who held to an acceptilation theory of the atonement and viewed faith (not in Christ's righteousness but in God's mercy apart from Christ's atonement) as a meritorious work of man. These deviations from the evangelical model of justification are in force today, although in somewhat less gross form. And we have all encountered them.

The Lutherans of the post-Reformation period and up to the present time have countered these aberrations in three ways. First, following Article II of the Formula of Concord, they show that man's receiving the grace of God in faith is itself a gift of grace, and that the absolution that forgives works the very faith to receive the forgiveness (Apol. XII, 39, passim). Secondly, they point out continually that faith's role in justification is purely instrumental, that faith is an *organon leptikon*, like the empty hand of a beggar receiving a gift, that it alone (*sola fide*) is the appropriate vehicle to receive reconciliation, forgiveness, Christ, and His merits (SD III, 30–38; Apol. IV, 163; AC XX, 28). Thirdly, they show that justification is *per fidem*, not *propter fidem*, by pointing out that faith justifies by virtue of its object, as Melanchthon used to say (Apol. IV, 56, 338, 227; SD III, 13), and that this is really only a different way of saying, "We are accounted righteous before God for Christ's sake through faith" (Apol. IV, 214).

[6] Bell (see chap. 2, n. 8), p. 29, writes:

Calvin never refers us to the use of the "practical syllogism" [= self-examination for assurance]. Even with regard to 2 Peter 1:10 (which was used by later Calvinists to justify the use of the practical syllogism), Calvin refuses to refer this to man's conscience as a means of determining the certainty of our salvation. He argues instead, that it means that one's calling (which in itself is certain) is confirmed "by a holy life." We do not look to our holiness for assurance of our salvation.

Rather, good works attest that "the sure foundation of a true and certain calling" has been laid in us by the Lord (see Calvin's Commentaries: 2Pe 1:10).

[7]Quoted from *Calvin's Commentaries: A Harmony of the Gospels Matthew, Mark, Luke, Volume III; and the Epistles of James and Jude*, trans. A. W. Morrison, ed. David W. Torrance and Thomas F. Torrance (Grand Rapids: Eerdmans, 1972), pp. 285–86.

Chapter 14

[1]See MacArthur, pp. 77–88. See also Walter Chantry's little volume (cited in chap. 1, n. 3), which is almost entirely devoted to a lordship treatment of the story of the rich young ruler.

[2]Of course, lordship teachers claim fidelity to the doctrine of John's gospel. But since John does not ever lay down "submission," "surrender," "sacrifice," or the like, as conditions for eternal life, lordship expositors are compelled to read their doctrine into John's text through a heavy-handed, invalid redefinition of saving faith. (See my discussion of this issue in chapter 2.)

[3]See my discussion of what it means to believe that Jesus is the Christ in chapter 3.

[4]Since eternal life is the very life of God himself, it is not to be viewed as a kind of "static entity" or as a "fixed quantity." Rather, its potentials are beyond human ability to calculate or define. So, as John 10:10 makes clear, eternal life can be possessed in varying degrees: i.e., one may "have life" and one may also "have it more abundantly."

The biblical teaching about eternal life is that this life is *not possessed at all* except as a divine gift bestowed on the one who believes. But the Bible also teaches that our experience of God's life can be enriched and enhanced. Thus one may even think of it as a reward granted at the end of the age to those who have sacrificially followed Christ. Indeed, eternal life is viewed as just such a recompense in Matthew 19:28–30; Mark 10:29–31; and Luke 18:29–30.

But an important distinction must be observed here if we are to remain true to the total teaching of God's Word. Very simply put, the distinction is this: No one can attain eternal life *as a reward*, who does not first receive it *as a free gift* by faith.

This vital differentiation is carefully observed by all the New Testament writers. All passages related to acquiring eternal life *here and now* condition it on faith alone. But passages treating it as a reward to be received for fidelity and sacrifice refer this reception *to the future.* Mark (10:30) and Luke (18:30) make this explicit with the phrase "in the age to come." By contrast, Jesus declared: "He who believes in Me *has* [here and now] everlasting life" (Jn 6:47; see esp. Jn 5:24).

The bottom line is this:

> If one does *not* believe in Christ for eternal life, he will "not see life" (Jn 3:36)—ever or in any degree.

> If he already possesses eternal life by faith, he can also possess it "more abundantly" (Jn 10:10)—i.e., he can acquire it as a future reward (Lk 18:30).

There is a ready analogy to all this which the Creator has built into the very fabric of *human life.* Every person born into the world possesses physical life as a gift—a bestowal—from his parents. He did nothing to earn or deserve it! But under the tutelage of capable parents and teachers, he can learn to develop this life, in its enormous potential, so that he can experience human life *more abundantly.*

This is precisely what we are called to do, for example, in a passage like 2 Peter 1:3–11, which we have looked at a number of times in this book. It should be noted, especially, that if we heed Peter's call to develop our new life in all its rich potential, the result will be *future reward*: ". . . for so an entrance will be supplied to you *abundantly* [= richly] into the everlasting kingdom of our Lord and Savior Jesus Christ" [2Pe 1:11; italics added].

Michael Green's treatment of 2 Peter 1:11 is excellent:

> This passage agrees with several in the Gospels and Epistles in suggesting that while heaven is entirely a gift of grace, it admits of degrees of felicity, and that these are dependent upon how faithfully we have built a structure of character and service upon the foundation of Christ. Bengel likens the unholy Christian in the judgment to a sailor who just manages to make shore after shipwreck, or to a man who barely escapes with his life from a burning house, while all his possessions are lost. In contrast, the Christian who has allowed his Lord to influence his conduct will have abundant entrance into the heavenly city, and be welcomed like a triumphant athlete victorious in the Games. This whole paragraph of exhortation is thus set between two poles: what we already are in Christ and what we are to become. The truly Christian reader, unlike the scoffers, will look back to the privileges conferred on him,

of partaking in the divine nature, and will seek to live worthily of it. He will also look forward to the day 'of assessment, and strive to live in the light of it.

Michael Green, *The Second Epistle General of Peter and the General Epistle of Jude: An Introduction and Commentary*, 2nd ed., Tyndale New Testament Commentaries, ed. Leon Morris (Grand Rapids: Eerdmans, 1987), p. 86.

[5] The words "for those who trust in riches" are not found in Aleph and B, two Greek manuscripts of the fourth century that are highly regarded by modern textual critics. A few other Greek manuscripts also omit the words. But the famous manuscripts, A, C, and D (all of the 5th century), include them, as does an overwhelming majority of the surviving Greek manuscripts of Mark. The rejection of the words "for those who trust in riches" by most modern editors and translators is extremely dubious, to say the least. The dropping of short phrases like this one (four words in Greek) is a well-known scribal failing. Moreover, Aleph and B share many common mistakes, as even their strong defenders usually admit.

Chapter 15

[1] Thus the Bauer-Gingrich-Danker lexicon (for bibliographic data, see chap. 2, n. 4) translates the phrase in Romans 10:10 this way: *"confess to salvation = so as to receive salvation"* (p. 229; italics in the original).

[2] See MacArthur, pp. 23, 190, 197. On page 190, MacArthur states in a footnote: "As a pastor, I take issue with Hodges' assertion that Paul was unconcerned about the destiny of members of the flocks he pastored." The word "unconcerned" has a pejorative ring to it. And, of course, I too am a pastor. My statement is found in *The Gospel Under Siege* (Dallas: Redención Viva, 1981), p. 95, where I affirm that Paul was not "constantly concerned about the eternal destiny of his readers."

MacArthur's response to me is inadequate for two reasons. (1) He is reading the modern church situation back into the New Testament. It has been estimated on the basis of the number of names mentioned in the greetings found in Romans 16:3–15, that the church at Rome itself was not likely to be much larger than about fifty people. And this must have been one of the larger congregations. If Paul did not know each member of his churches personally, the elders of each church did. It was quite easy for New Testament church leaders to find out whether or not an individual understood and believed the gospel in congregations as small as New Testament churches usually were.

But this leads us to (2). MacArthur's own doctrine of faith and assurance does not even permit the believer himself to know for sure whether he has truly believed. So how could a pastor find out if a person does, without watching that person's behavior over a long period of time? And even then, the pastor could not be sure just as the believer himself could not be sure, since perseverance to the end is required!

But Paul did not preach the sort of gospel that creates this kind of uncertainty and doubt. Paul knew that the Philippian jailer and his family were saved the very night they believed and, accordingly, he baptized them that same night (Ac 16:33)! If there is any significant number of people in our congregations today who are actually unsaved, the fault is ours for not preaching the gospel clearly and for not making sure that each individual understands and believes it.

But such faults are not to be laid at the feet of Paul or of Pauline-trained church elders! They preached and taught a clear gospel of faith and assurance, and they did so "publicly and from house to house" (Ac 20:20).

Subject Index

Scripture Index

234
H689
C.2

LINCOLN CHRISTIAN COLLEGE AND SEMINARY

113971

3 4711 00183 6271